the
Volleyball
Drill Book

AMERICAN VOLLEYBALL
COACHES ASSOCIATION

Teri Clemens

Jenny McDowell

avca
AMERICAN VOLLEYBALL
COACHES ASSOCIATION

Human Kinetics

Library of Congress Cataloging-in-Publication Data

The volleyball drill book / American Volleyball Coaches Association ; [edited by] Teri Clemens, Jenny McDowell.
    p. cm.
  ISBN 978-1-4504-2386-1 (soft cover) -- ISBN 1-4504-2386-8 (soft cover)
1. Volleyball--Training. 2. Volleyball--Coaching. I. Clemens, Teri, 1956- II. McDowell, Jenny.
III. American Volleyball Coaches Association.
  GV1015.5.T73V645 2012
  796.325--dc23

                    2012005987

ISBN-10: 1-4504-2386-8 (print)
ISBN-13: 978-1-4504-2386-1 (print)

Acquisitions Editor: Justin Klug; **Developmental Editor:** Carla Zych; **Assistant Editor:** Claire Marty; **Copyeditor:** Annette Pierce; **Graphic Designers:** Bob Reuther and Nancy Rasmus; **Graphic Artist:** Kim McFarland; **Cover Designer:** Keith Blomberg; **Photographer (cover):** Toshifumi/AFP/Getty Images; **Photographer (interior):** Kay Hinton, Emory Photo/Video; **Visual Production Assistant:** Joyce Brumfield; **Photo Production Manager:** Jason Allen; **Art Manager:** Kelly Hendren; **Associate Art Manager:** Alan L. Wilborn; **Illustrations:** © Human Kinetics; **Printer:** United Graphics

We thank Emory University in Atlanta, Georgia, for assistance in providing the photos for this book.

Human Kinetics books are available at special discounts for bulk purchase. Special editions or book excerpts can also be created to specification. For details, contact the Special Sales Manager at Human Kinetics.

Printed in the United States of America   10   9   8   7   6   5   4   3   2   1

The paper in this book is certified under a sustainable forestry program.

Human Kinetics
Website: www.HumanKinetics.com

United States: Human Kinetics
P.O. Box 5076
Champaign, IL 61825-5076
800-747-4457
e-mail: humank@hkusa.com

Canada: Human Kinetics
475 Devonshire Road Unit 100
Windsor, ON N8Y 2L5
800-465-7301 (in Canada only)
e-mail: info@hkcanada.com

Europe: Human Kinetics
107 Bradford Road
Stanningley
Leeds LS28 6AT, United Kingdom
+44 (0) 113 255 5665
e-mail: hk@hkeurope.com

Australia: Human Kinetics
57A Price Avenue
Lower Mitcham, South Australia 5062
08 8372 0999
e-mail: info@hkaustralia.com

New Zealand: Human Kinetics
P.O. Box 80
Torrens Park, South Australia 5062
0800 222 062
e-mail: info@hknewzealand.com

E5645

*We dedicate this book to all the passionate and dedicated coaches
who strive to help their teams reach their full potential
by creating and adapting drills to fit the needs of their programs.*

Contents

Drill Finder

Drill title	Level	Serving	Ball Handling	Setting	Offense	Defense	Transition	Competition	Mental Toughness & Team Building	Page #
CHAPTER 2										
Serving Ladder	●	X								12
Caterpillar Serving	●	X								14
Minute-to-Win-It Serving	●	X								16
Run to Serve	●	X								18
Serve and Catch	●	X								20
Four-Square Serving	●	X								22
Tic-Tac-Toe	●●	X								23
Zone Challenge	●●	X								24
H-O-R-S-E Serving Competition	●●	X								25
Quads Serve and Pass	●●	X								26
Quad Serving Competition	●●	X								28
Serve Bonus Triples	●●●	X								29
CHAPTER 3										
Minute-to-Win-It Passing	●		X							34
Control Passing	●		X							36
Libero Serve–Pass Challenge	●●		X							38
3-2-1 Passing	●●		X							40
Four-Person Pepper	●●		X							42
Pounce (Bounce and Pass)	●●		X							44
Zigzag Passing	●●		X							46
Shank You!	●●		X							48
Long-Court Pepper Challenge	●●		X							49
Transition Passing	●●		X							50
Long-Court Cooperative Challenge	●●		X							52
Texas Star Drill	●●		X							53
30-Second Pepper Switch	●●		X							54
Pass Out	●●●		X							55
Chaos Passing	●●●		X							56
Team Cooperative Rally	●●●		X							58

(continued)

Drill Finder

Drill title	Level	Serving	Ball Handling	Setting	Offense	Defense	Transition	Competition	Mental Toughness & Team Building	Page #
CHAPTER 6 (CONTINUED)										
Three-Gun Salute	🏐					X				116
Check Your Distance	🏐					X				117
Out of the Net	🏐					X				118
Under-the-Net Digging	🏐					X				119
Block, Hit, Block	🏐					X				120
Defensive Tango	🏐					X				122
21-Gun Salute	🏐🏐					X				124
Scramble	🏐🏐					X				125
Defensive-Priority Response System	🏐🏐					X				126
Dig a Dozen	🏐🏐					X				128
Right-Side Unity Drill	🏐🏐					X				130
Figure 8	🏐🏐					X				132
Overpass Challenge	🏐🏐					X				134
Blind Blocking	🏐🏐					X				136
Three-Person Positional Pepper	🏐🏐					X				137
Defense or Bust	🏐🏐🏐					X				138
CHAPTER 7										
Pull Drill	🏐						X			143
Single-Defender Reaction Challenge	🏐🏐						X			144
Focus on Skills—No Ball	🏐🏐						X			145
Team Transition	🏐🏐						X			146
Triples Transition	🏐🏐						X			148
Transition or Bust	🏐🏐						X			150
Free-Ball, Down-Ball Quick Attack	🏐🏐🏐						X			152
Team Defensive Movement	🏐🏐🏐						X			154
End-It-Quickly Team Transition	🏐🏐🏐						X			156
Outside-Hitter Transitional Pepper	🏐🏐🏐						X			158

(continued)

Drill Finder *(continued)*

Drill title	Level	Serving	Ball Handling	Setting	Offense	Defense	Transition	Competition	Mental Toughness & Team Building	Page #
CHAPTER 9 (CONTINUED)										
Two-Minute, Free-Ball Frenzy	●●●							X		208
Serve, Down Ball, Free Ball	●●●							X		210
Bongo	●●●							X		211
Back-Row, One vs. One Challenge	●●●							X		212
CHAPTER 10										
Team Song	●								X	218
Chain Story	●								X	219
Bulletin Board	●								X	220
I Was Wondering	●								X	221
I Am Competitive	●								X	222
Whatever	●								X	224
Hammer	●●								X	225
Team Challenge	●●								X	226
You Want; They Want	●●								X	227
You Got Game?	●●								X	228
Attention to Detail	●●●								X	229
Be Positive!	●●●								X	230
Risk City	●●●								X	231
You Wanna Know Why We Win?	●●●								X	232
Winners and Whiners	All								X	234
Celebrity Double Trouble	All								X	236

Preface

What makes a good coach? We all know the short answer: good players.

So maybe we need to reframe the question: Why do some coaches always seem to have good players? No matter where they coach, no matter what the level, no matter what the gender, they always have good players.

How is this possible? Some would credit specific training techniques, although there are plenty of good teams that have developed under quite different philosophical systems. Some would cite feeder programs, although we can all name teams that fail to win in spite of generous pipelines. Still others might say that elite athletes make the difference, yet teams stocked with acclaimed athletes often fail to win championships.

The fundamental truth is that good coaches are good teachers. In volleyball this means they talk very little and their players touch the ball a lot; they train with a purpose and let their players know what is expected of them; they make players better and that means their players enjoy being in the gym.

The currency for good coaches is drills. We seem to know this instinctively. At every clinic I have ever attended or conducted the most popular sessions have been those with the word 'drills' in the title. Regardless of the skill level of the attendees or the resume of the presenter, the word *drills* is a magnet for volleyball coaches. We are drawn to them like bees to pollen, kids to candy, and moths to light. We are predictable, insatiable, addicted. We look to drills to cure whatever ails us. Drills are our lifeline to credibility as we begin coaching, the spark for new enthusiasm when we grow bored, and the touchstone for creativity as we mature. Drills are the drug of choice in coaching.

So what better book for the AVCA to produce than one that engages great teacher-coaches and that focuses completely and specifically on drills? We knew from the start that Emory University coach Jenny McDowell and former Washington University coach Teri Clemens were the perfect duo to author this book. Not only have they both won national championships, they have collected numerous Coach of the Year awards, they have worked with both beginners and All-Americans, they understand the phases of the coaching life cycle, and they are incorrigible drill-seekers themselves.

Teri and Jenny recognize that the main cause of our addiction to drills is time, or, more accurately, the lack of it. All coaches are short on practice hours. We must teach skills, coordinate strategies, and mold a group of individuals into a team, all in far less time than we'd like. Drills help us focus our efforts; they allow us to concentrate on problem areas and target weaknesses for added attention.

Coaches know intuitively that players, particularly in their formative years, learn by doing. As much as we are all looking for a passing pill or setting epiphany, the truth is that it takes a mind-numbingly large number of repetitions to gain proficiency in these and other basic skills. Drills give us the tools to ward off the inevitable boredom by providing fresh ways to practice the same old skills.

I'll close with some final words on what makes *The Volleyball Drill Book* unique.

First, because of its specific focus, this book contains more drills than any other volleyball book. Veteran coaches looking for variety and new ways to practice will find everything they need right here. Coaches with less experience will want to partner this book with the AVCA's *Volleyball Skills and Drills,* which outlines fundamental techniques and teaching cues.

Second, *The Volleyball Drill Book* is written for coaches of both genders and all levels. There are drills for beginning, intermediate, and advanced players, and the authors offer suggestions for modifying the drills to make them either less or more challenging.

Third, each drill is explained, organized, and illustrated in a similar fashion, using consistent symbols and easy-to-decipher diagrams. This frees coaches to coach, rather than simply enter balls or keep score.

Learning to coach is a process, just like learning to play. Good coaches develop their skills with practice, with intentional focus on improvement and evaluation of their strengths and weaknesses. The tools of our trade are drills. This book is like a paint-by-numbers canvas; the outlines were created by experts, the colors and textures are up to you. Enjoy!

Kathy DeBoer
AVCA Executive Director

Acknowledgments

We are grateful to

Kathy DeBoer and the AVCA, for their support in making this book a reality;

Carla Zych and the rest of the staff at Human Kinetics, who worked closely with us on this project;

Justin Hart, who reviewed and typed for us, putting in countless hours in the preparation stages;

Linda Adams, Sid Feldman, Jim Iams, Mike Larko, Kathy Major, and Ellen Toy, our own former coaches, who have impacted our coaching and even more significantly, our lives; and

Amanda Welter and Joe Worlund, our long time friends and assistants, whose loyalty has been unmatched.

We send a special salute to all of our former players from Washington University in St. Louis and Emory University, who have competitively, tirelessly, and patiently performed our drills over the years. We love you all!

Key to Diagrams

A	Attacker
B	Blocker
C	Coach
D	Digger or defender
F	Feeder
H	Hitter
L	Libero
LB	Left-back player
LF	Left-front player
LFB	Left-front blocker
MB	Middle-back player
MF	Middle-front player
MFB	Middle-front blocker
MH	Middle hitter
OH	Outside hitter
OP	Opposite or right-side hitter
P	Passer
RB	Right-back player
RF	Right-front player
RFB	Right-front blocker
S	Setter
SS	Scorekeeper
Sv	Server
T	Target
Ts	Tosser
X	Any player, when position isn't important

A	Side A
B	Side B
△	Cone
⟶	Path of player
- - →	Path of ball
·······►	Path of imaginary ball
🏐	Ball cart
☐	Empty ball cart
▢	Platform
)	Shagger

chapter 1

Integrating Drills Into Practice

"Coach, can we run that again?"

"That was *awesome*!"

"Wow, that was close! Let's do it again. We'll take you."

"It seems like the drill just started."

"The time is flying by today!"

"Thanks, Coach!"

Are these the type of comments being made in your gym during practice? Is this the level of enthusiasm your players bring to matches? If not, we can help.

Drills are the essence of a strong practice and the foundation for a strong team. Drills can be cooperative and competitive or both, and with some advance planning, they can be well organized, well run, and well received.

Effective, enjoyable practices take place in a safe, efficient, and clean environment. Practices should be inviting and should include a comfortable welcome and a routine warm-up that brings players together and prepares them to work as a team. Coaches and players should have high expectations that each practice will include opportunities for achievement, improvement, camaraderie, and yes, *fun*!

It is essential to establish that players are winners before starting a practice. The success rate for the drills is be higher when coaches make it clear that they believe in the players and expect them to be successful in the drills.

Coach, you are ultimately responsible for the motivation of your team. You must demand the best from yourself, and deliver it, before you can demand a high standard of performance from your players. If players believe in you and know you believe in them, they will believe in themselves. If you *sell* the drills, your players will *buy* the drills.

To select the right drills for your team you must know yourself and your team. To make the drills work you must plan ahead so that you can make the most of your practice time.

To keep practices interesting, you must be creative, innovative, or both, and you must have the ability to adapt drills to meet the needs of your team. The drills outlined in this book can be used as presented or can be readily adapted to your program. There are no rules! Change any part of any drill to mix things up or to better meet the needs of your players.

Planning

Most of us coaches have spent summers and weekends thinking about the season with every intention of being completely prepared ahead of time with a detailed season calendar containing planned practices and drills. Shoot, we may have had the victories on the scoreboard already and patted ourselves on the back for all our early preparation and insight. But despite our *dreamin' and schemin'* many of us have also seen reality set in the weekend before preseason, when a last-minute blood pressure spike or a bout of nausea reminded us that we had failed to develop our rough ideas into focused plans and put them on paper.

A good first step toward developing a season plan is to consider your coaching and support staff. You'll want to take full advantage of any assistants you may have and the skills they have to offer. Decide how to use your assistants before the start of practice and adjust this plan as needed during practice.

Think about your players, both as individuals and as a team. Evaluate their knowledge of the game, their skills, and their strengths and weaknesses. Consider their physical and emotional maturity and their learning styles as you select drills and activities to challenge them.

Evaluate your coaching and communication style. Making your expectations clear extends beyond issues of performance and discipline. If you want your players to learn to be self-motivated and to develop leadership skills of their own, create opportunities for them to do so.

Drill Selection

Once you have established the direction of your program and have in mind what you want to achieve in a season, you can begin to develop the general practice scheme for a season. Both coach-centered drills and player-centered drills should be used. In coach-centered drills, a coach is directly involved. The coach provides instruction, controls the pace, and initiates the ball. This type of drill is most often used in the instructional phase early in the season. In player-centered drills, players initiate the ball and control the pace, and the coach's role is to provide feedback and teach as needed. Because a player initiates the ball in match play, it is important to include this type of drill most often.

Putting together the drills for a particular practice is not a mindless or random process in which you drop in just enough drills to fill a time slot. The needs of the team and the type of opposition they will face must be considered. These factors change over the course of the season; therefore, your practice plans must change.

Preseason drills should offer many repetitions so players can learn and practice skills. The total number of touches (times a player touches the volleyball) should be much higher during this phase than in any other time of the season. Choose drills that afford a lot of touches for each player. Preseason is a time for teaching and for conducting technical checkups on various skills in both individual and group play. Advanced teams, as well as beginning teams, are in learning mode, although at different levels. A high number of touches is necessary at this time, and the repetitions will pay off all season long.

The fact that this is a time for learning does not mean that preseason drills should not offer competition. Quite the opposite! Get players' competitive fire stoked early—as early as day one. Competitions for doubles, triples, and quads allow players many more touches than 6v6 team competitions. Preseason is the perfect time for these mini team games.

Focus more on individual drill selections and less on the multiplayer or team selections during the preseason. Practices tend to be longer to allow for skill repetition, so change drills often to keep players interested. Repeat the skills, not the drills!

Midseason is the time to rely on offense, defense, transition, multiplayer, and team drills. While there is still a need for skill repetition, it requires less emphasis than in preseason. The bigger goal is to heighten preparation for team play and match opposition. Team emphasis and strong transition work is key during this time. Work on free-ball plays and play short scoring games with many opportunities for players to experience victory. This encourages the desire to win. The focus at this stage is more on *team* than individual players. Nearly all drills should have a gamelike competitive quality.

Postseason practices are usually shorter and therefore must be extremely efficient. You must be precise in your drill selection because you are now preparing specifically for each opponent, addressing in more detail what the team will face in upcoming matches than you did in midseason. Address opposition matchups within team drills and set up competition to mimic opposition as closely as possible. Beginning teams may need to continue to focus on their own side of the net because their goals and approach to the game will vary only minimally based on the skills and strategies of their opponents.

In every season, each practice should begin with a warm-up, progress through several drills, climax with a well-organized competition section, and wind down to a satisfying ending, just like a well-written book. Remember, Coach, volleyball is all about practice and improvement! Matches are played just so we know what to work on at the next practice!

Repetition

Determining how much repetition is too much can be difficult. Most coaches struggle with two questions:

1. How many times do we repeat a drill in a season?
2. How many times do we repeat the skill within a drill?

Keep in mind that players come to practice to play. Some coaches get caught up in extensive explanation, and the drill can lose its magic before it begins. Keep instructions brief and clear and let players learn by playing.

There's nothing better than hearing, "Let's go again!" It can be tempting to give in to players' pleas for more, but it's always best to leave them hungry. Take that energy into another drill.

Day-to-day practices must include a wide range of activities. Drills should be inviting and exciting so that players are eager to come to practice each day. Let players be inspired by the creative drills you offer.

It is a good practice to have a handful of drills that you repeat throughout a season. But in the long run, players accomplish more if you offer a constantly changing variety of drills. The challenge of a new drill often awakens a spirit of enthusiasm, even if the same skills are being used.

We've probably all overdone a good thing. The ideal time to end a drill is *before* the players and coaches tire of it.

Finally, remember this: Many repetitions in a short time are more valuable than a few repetitions over a long time. In other words, keep the lines short in drills, Coach. No one wants to stand in a long line, and your feedback isn't as effective if a player doesn't get to act on it right away with another try. This is beneficial to the rhythm of a drill also—drills typically flow better with a small group. But the next small group should be ready, and the transition time between groups should be short. A good rule of thumb is to have no more than three players in a line. Just change the groups often.

Making the Most of Each Practice

You have evaluated your team. You have selected drills. You might be able to read it and run it! But remember, you may need to make adaptations within the drill to meet your needs or your number of players. Give yourself time. Prepare in advance who will be in the groups or on the teams, who will substitute where and when, and what pace you will maintain throughout a drill. Is a reward necessary for winners? Try rewarding winners with more of the same! For example, the winner of a triples match gets to play triples against three coaches, or the winner of a blocking competition gets 10 extra blocks. This type of reward not only encourages individual players, but it also helps the team.

The staff in your gym must be organized with an efficient plan to run drills. Tossing, hitting, and serving are necessary skills for staff members directly involved in running the drills. Coaches and tossers must know (and may need to practice) all the methods of entering balls into drills. Popping balls into play underhand or overhead with a half-swing in order to reduce the wear on a shoulder will give you many more years of involvement. Tossing well is something of a lost art, and doing it while continuously receiving balls from a feeder can be challenging. You may have to arrive early to practice . . . to practice!

Coaches must train themselves to pay attention to the task at hand. During a passing drill, give feedback on passing. If the pass leads to a great set and a kill terminates the play, *give feedback on the pass*. This takes practice. The natural tendency is to follow the action to termination and comment on the end result. Physically positioning yourself so that the specific skill you're working on is your main visual focus may help.

Nurturing the Competitive Edge

Players become more competitive if they are given more competitive opportunities. Do more drills that use a scoring system than drills that don't. Scorekeeping adds a gamelike pressure and generally raises the level of play. Only in cooperative drills that serve instructional purposes should you not keep score. Competitions can be rather basic, such as in counting the number of passes to a target. Or they can be much more advanced, such as scoring in serve-receive, free-ball and defensive transition—all to get just 1 point. It is the coach's responsibility to encourage the joy of competition by showing eagerness to see players achieve the reward. We, as coaches, must nurture the desire to win and the desire to win again. Praise players; actively support their quest for victory even in the simplest competition. Do it with spirit and show some emotion. Slapping hands or allowing time for a quick mini-celebration on the court is important. Encourage this connection—remember that this connection is the reason many players compete in team sports. Allow players who are naturally competitive to lead in this area!

Scoring goals for drills should most often be low. A 6v6 team drill will usually be more effective if it ends at 6 to 9 points rather than continuing to 25. Shorter contests offer many more opportunities for victories over the course of a practice or season. Remember, we want to provide many opportunities for success. The more players win, the more they will desire the feelings that winning brings. Short games also allow for easy substitutions and make scorekeeping simpler. Finally, they provide multiple opportunities for water breaks and performance feedback.

As you work your way through the remaining chapters and plan your practice sessions, keep these coaching points in mind:

- Players really do follow the leader. If you prepare, they will prepare. If you compete, they will compete. If you believe in a drill, they will believe in a drill. If you sell it, they will buy it!
- Establish a method for organizing drills within a practice and plan ahead.
- Select and adapt the drills to fit the needs of your players.
- Allow fun to happen. A sense of humor is a must. Let players enjoy the moment, then get them back on task.

- Use variety and competition to inspire your players.
- Remember that unexpected events during practice help players learn how to handle those events in matches. If the team prepares for surprises, there are no surprises!

chapter 2

Serving Drills

The serve is not just a method to initiate play in volleyball. Consider it the first offensive weapon of the game. A team has to serve to win. No way around it, Coach. Adding pace and movement to the serve often makes it more difficult for the passers to handle it. An aggressive server can disrupt even the finest of offenses on the opposing side of the net. A strong server can make even a great hitter less effective by disrupting the pass, which means fewer options for the setter. A disrupted set then causes problems for the hitter, often creating a situation that prevents a great swing on the hit. Thus, when playing teams with good offensive weapons, the serve becomes even more important.

How much risk should a player take when serving? The answer lies somewhere between the amount of consistency in that serve and the ability of the offense on the opposing side. It is certainly important to get the ball in, but it's also important not to serve a ball that is so easily handled that the opposing offense can swing away at will. The server should move to the endline, face the target, and essentially serve the same way each time.

> We jokingly tell players "if you sneeze before you serve the first time in a season, you'd better sneeze the rest of the season."
>
> Although we do not really demand such extreme discipline, this statement makes the point that we expect them to develop and use a consistent routine.

There are three steps to the serve: the presentation, the toss in front of the hitting shoulder, and the follow-through to the target. Each phase must be performed correctly. Check players' technique before drills, and do checkups during and after to be sure that players are executing each step properly.

It is imperative to not only teach the serve skill but to run serving drills and to develop pride in being an effective serving team. Individual goals and team goals are good incentives. Simply adding a bonus point for an ace to a competition in a multiplayer or team drill helps players recognize its value and encourages them to give it their best effort.

Start keeping statistics so players know when a serve is effective. Have you ever asked a server after a long rally in a drill what the opposition did with the serve? Did the server recall? A server should know what disruption, if any, the serve caused.

Tracking the serve and what the opponent does with the serve (such as who passes, how effective the pass is, and if it results in a kill) helps us to know what is working. Players can watch to see whether their own serve is causing disruption within the passing system across the net. Does the passer have to move? Does the pass make the setter move? Does the setter have four options, two options, one, or zero? It is a good practice to help players learn to observe the results of a serve.

The ABC method works well for beginners. Serves are identified as A, B, and C. A is an average serve—one that can be counted on when the team needs the serve in the court. It is in the court 95 percent of the time. B is a better serve. It is more aggressive than A and less aggressive than C. C is for crank it! It is an opportunity to go for it. Many players respond well to this system. It is an effective method for letting young players have freedom without losing control of the serve. If you choose to use this system, try it in drills. A coach could assign a progression of serving an A, then B, then C, and then have players repeat the sequence. Another example is to serve B, C, B, C. Or simply use an A as the first serve in a match, and after time-outs, delays, the start of a new game, and so on. Some drills in this book use this method.

Many drills within this chapter request players to hit to particular zones. Typically, the court is divided into six zones, numbered by position, so that zone 1 is an area of the court where the opposing server plays, and so on. If you plan to call the service zones during matches, make sure to call them (or have someone else call them) during practice so that players become familiar with the calls. This makes players more comfortable and less likely to panic when the calls are made during a match.

Coach, accept that no player tries to make an error. This may surprise the parents in the stands, who often moan and groan over a missed serve at any time during the match. Players must understand the back-to-back rule of thumb, however. Simply said, although players are bound to miss occasionally, they should not miss back to back with their own last serve, with the serve before them on their own team, or the last serve from the opposing team. Following this simple guideline during drills makes players much more alert in games. Just remind them when they are making a serve in a back-to-back situation. If your players understand this system, nothing more needs to be said.

Keep these points in mind when coaching serving drills:

- Use competition in serving drills to motivate your players.
- Teach players to be attentive to whether the serve disrupts the offense within drills.
- Players should have a purpose in mind before each serve. Is it an A, B, or C situation? Should the serve go to zone 3? Deep? Short?
- As the coach, you should be as focused during serving drills as in any drill. Paying close attention sends the message to players that serving is an important skill.
- Emphasize that the presentation affects the consistency of the serve.

SERVING LADDER

Purpose

To introduce deep-zone serving in a competitive environment where servers advance based on score.

Setup

The coach creates a round-robin tournament in which each player plays every other player. Players compete in pairs assigned by the coach. The first pair, a server and a feeder, sets up at the service line with a basket of balls. To keep things moving quickly, a pair of players can be in position at each corner of the court, ready to start. The court area on both sides of the net is divided into six zones, numbered by player position and marked with cones or tape.

Run the Drill

1. Players compete one pair at a time. The player who is serving attempts to serve six balls in order to the designated location: two balls to zone 1, two balls to zone 6, and two balls to zone 5.
2. The server earns 3 points for a serve into the correct zone, 1 point for a serve into any other zone, and 0 points for a missed serve or serving error. The server is allowed one free miss.
3. The server's partner feeds balls to the server and calls out the score after each serve. Shaggers collect the balls in a basket.
4. At the end of the sequence; the partners switch roles. When both players have finished serving, the pair leaves the court, and the player with the higher score reports the winning score to the coach.
5. The coach signals the next pair (already in position on the court) to begin and assigns a new pair of players to the empty corner to wait their turn. Each time a new pair begins, the shaggers swap the full and empty carts so that the new players start with a full basket. Play continues until every player has played every other player.

Coaching Points

- Set a fast pace. The drill is intended to be short to put more emphasis on the importance of each serve.
- A play-off with the top four finishers gives a great incentive.

Variations

- Allow two or three misses to encourage a go-for-it attitude.
- Have players serve 8 or 10 balls per round.
- Have players serve 6 balls, 2 to each short zone (2, 3, and 4).

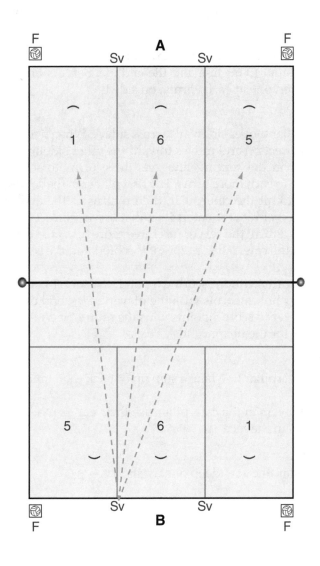

Purpose

To improve serving accuracy by serving at a target made up of moving players.

Setup

Two groups of three players link arms to form a "caterpillar" and set up on side A between the 10-foot (3 m) line and the endline. Servers line up behind the endline in two lines, one at each corner, on side B.

Run the Drill

1. Each caterpillar moves sideways across side A. When it touches a sideline, it reverses direction and moves toward the other sideline.
2. Each player in the serving line gets three turns to serve and has the opportunity to earn more turns. The first player in the serving line serves, attempting to hit the caterpillar, then returns to the end of the serving line. If the server hits the caterpillar, that serve scores 1 point and it does not count as a turn; the server has three more turns to score. If the server does not hit the caterpillar, no point is scored and the server has used up one turn.
3. After three turns without scoring a point, the server becomes part of the caterpillar by linking arms with the player on the end of the caterpillar.
4. The first player to score 5 points wins the round. Servers and caterpillars switch roles for the next round.

Coaching Points

- Have the caterpillar line take a step up or back each time the line reaches the sideline.
- Have the players in the caterpillar use their hands to keep the ball from hitting them in the face.

Variation

Have the caterpillar line stay deep or stay short.

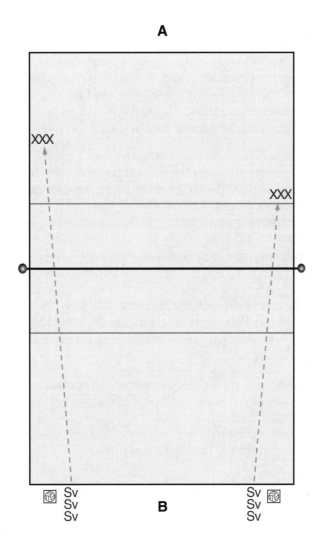

Purpose

To improve the percentages of successful serves by serving to various zones.

Setup

Both sides of the court are divided into zones based on player position. The zone borders are marked with cones, tape, or jump ropes. A supply of balls is placed near the serving position on each side of the court. Three servers line up at each serving position. At least three shaggers get into position on each side of the court; one sets up near the endline and the others spread out across the court. The coach sets a clock or timer to 60 seconds.

Run the Drill

1. The first server in each line chooses a zone or the coach assigns a zone.
2. At the coach's signal, the first server in the line serves and counts the number of serves that land in the given zone.
3. The shaggers on the court retrieve the balls and relay them to the shagger on the endline near the basket.
4. After one minute, the coach signals the server to stop. The server reports the score to the coach, and the first player in the other serving line takes a turn.
5. When all the servers in each line have taken a turn, the servers and shaggers switch places. Play continues until every player has taken a turn. The player who puts the most serves in the designated zone wins.

Coaching Points

- To increase speed and efficiency, a feeder can bounce a ball to the server. The feeder must pay attention and be ready to deliver as soon as the server turns for a ball.
- The fast-paced competitive feel is part of the fun. Use two coaches and two timers to reduce the time between turns.

Variations

- Add passers and a setter who catches the pass or sets to a hitter or target who catches it.
- Keep score as a team. Add the scores of the six servers on the court versus the next six servers.
- Focus on one zone or a small number of zones throughout the drill or change the zone during the drill.

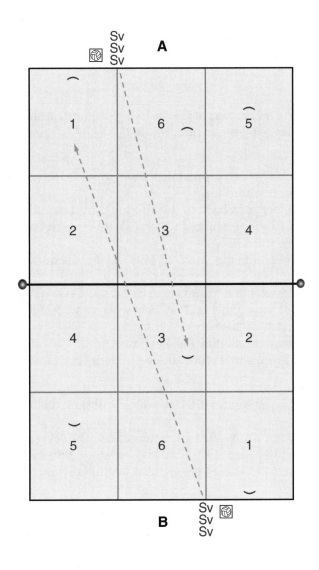

The "running to the endline" aspect of this drill gives the players a gamelike feel at practice.

Purpose

To practice serving under gamelike conditions by running back to serve, turning, and serving.

Setup

Three sets of three servers start at the 10-foot (3 m) line on side A. Each group has three balls. Shaggers spread out on side B.

Run the Drill

1. The first player in each group takes a ball, runs to the endline, turns, and serves within five seconds.
2. The same player runs back to the 10-foot (3 m) line, is handed a second ball, runs back to the endline, and serves within the five-second time limit. Repeat for the third ball.
3. The second player in the group repeats the same sequence with the three balls.
4. The third player in the group repeats the sequence with the three balls. As a group of three finishes, it switches places with the shaggers so that everyone has an equal chance to compete.
5. The goal is to make all nine balls in a row.
6. Reward the groups that score all nine in their second round.

Coaching Points

- Encourage players to run full out, which will train them to move quickly in matches.
- Players may not throw the ball to the server. The server must run all the way back to the 10-foot (3 m) line and be handed the ball.
- Encourage players, except those at the beginner level, to serve tough.

Variations

- Practice serving to specific zones. Once a player runs back to the endline and gets set to serve, have a member of that player's group assign a zone to which the player has to serve. This makes the drill more like a game.
- Once a group of three misses two serves, the group must stop and a new group comes on to replace it.

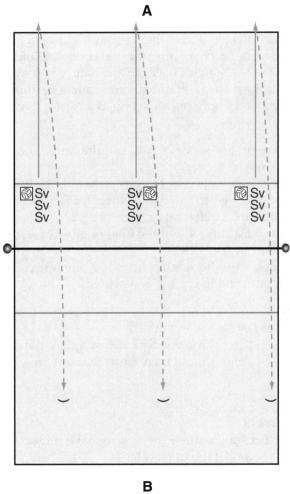

Purpose

To increase both the pace and accuracy of the serve.

Setup

Servers line up behind the endline on side A next to a cart of balls. One catcher sets up on the court on side B, and the rest of the catchers line up behind the endline on that side. The coach sets up near the service line and counts all serves, including missed ones. A second coach, an assistant, or a player sets up behind the endline on side B next to a cart of balls and counts the number of aces. Any ball *not* caught by an opposing player acting as a catcher is considered an ace.

Run the Drill

1. The first server in line serves a ball, and the catcher attempts to catch it, regardless of where it goes.
2. Once the ball lands or is caught, the catcher places it in the basket. The server and catcher go to the end of their respective lines, and the next server and the next catcher take a turn.
3. The coaches count and call out the total number of serves and aces with each serve and catch.
4. Play continues until the serving team has attempted 25 serves. Players then switch roles and the action is repeated.

Coaching Points

- Keep the pace fast.
- Make sure that players use good form throughout the drill. Their consistency and confidence should increase as the drill progresses. It is fun for all levels.

Variations

- Use two catchers.
- Use two catchers and require the first to make contact with the ball and pass it to the second, who must catch it.

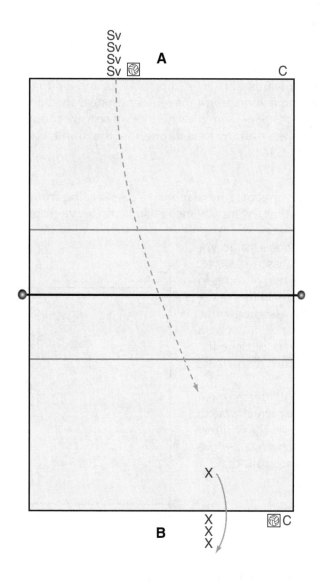

Purpose

To enable beginners to learn to serve accurately into large zones.

Setup

Each side of the court is divided in half, using lines, tape, cones, markers, or jump ropes. Four teams of two or three players and a supply of balls are on the endline behind a zone. Extra players set up near the back of each zone to serve as shaggers. One person in each group of servers counts accurate serves as points and keeps a running total throughout the round. For each round, two minutes are on the clock.

Run the Drill

1. Beginning teams may have more success serving from only one side of the net at a time. More advanced teams can serve from both ends at the same time.
2. The coach chooses a down-the-line or crosscourt serve.
3. Teams have two minutes to serve as many balls as possible in the assigned zone, one player per team at a time. Shaggers retrieve the balls and return them to the basket.
4. The team that puts the most serves in the correct zone in two minutes is the winner.
5. Teams switch zone assignments for each round.

Coaching Points

- Encourage players to initiate the serve the same way every time.
- As players improve, begin calling zone 1 or zone 2 to servers. This helps improve overall serve control. Players can later advance to more zones.

Variation

Have players compete only against the other players in their group. Winners advance to a special group to play for overall champion.

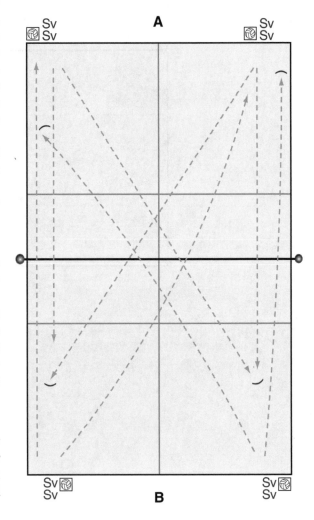

TIC-TAC-TOE

Purpose

To increase accuracy by serving to specific areas on the court.

Setup

The coaches use cones or tape to mark out nine equal zones on each side of the court. A basket of balls is placed at each endline. The coach sets aside a group of objects to mark the zones as players score there (alternatively, extra players can sit in the zones to mark them). A team of three players sets up behind each endline. Shaggers set up at the sidelines.

Run the Drill

1. At the coach's signal, the first player in each line serves, then goes to the back of the serving line.
2. When a zone is hit, the coach marks it. A shagger retrieves the ball and places it in one of the baskets.
3. Play continues with players in both groups serving by turns, attempting to claim more zones. The goal for each team is to claim three zones in a row in any direction to win the round.
4. After each round, replace the groups of three so that everyone gets to play. Keep a win–loss record for each team.

Coaching Points

- Introduce players to zone serving before running the drill; otherwise, their success will be lucky rather than being earned.
- As the players improve, accept only well-hit balls. Allow no wimpy serving.

Variations

- Have teams compete to win two rounds out of three.
- Add passers and setters on each side as the servers continue to try for tic-tac-toe.
- Require a specific type of three in a row in order to win, such as diagonal only.

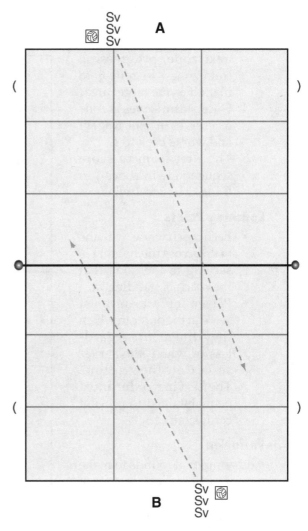

Purpose

To improve accuracy of serving to specific areas of the court.

Setup

Teams of two to six servers set up at each endline, each with a ball in hand. A designated shagger sets up next to the cart of balls near each serving line. The coach marks out six zones on each side with tape, lines, or ropes. A coach or player serving as the target marker stands in zone 1.

Run the Drill

1. The first player in each line serves to zone 1 on the opposite side and then goes to the end of the serving line.
2. Players in the serving line take turns serving, one player from each line at a time.
3. As soon as an acceptable serve enters the target zone, the coach or player in that zone moves to the next zone, progressing from zone 1 to zone 6, to mark it as the target area.
4. Once a team serves in zone 6, it serves in zone 6 again and works back to 1.
5. The first team to score sequentially in zones 1 to 6 and then 6 to 1 wins.

Coaching Points

- Each coach works with the team across the net that is serving to the zone that the coach is standing in.
- Players on a team must serve in the order in which they lined up, regardless of where the server serves on the endline. The serving order must be maintained to prevent confusion.

Variation

Add additional rounds to make the competition best two out of three. Follow the same sequence: 1 to 6 then 6 to 1 and repeat two or three times.

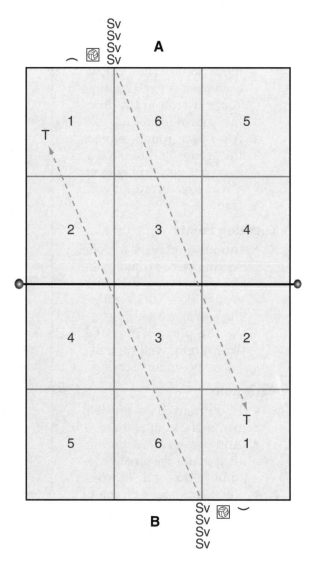

Purpose

To practice serving to the different zones on the court.

Setup

The court is divided into the six player-position zones with floor tape or cones or in some other way. Two teams of two set up on both endlines; one team will serve, and the other will shag. Position a cart of balls off the court at the endlines.

Run the Drill

1. This drill is like the game of horse in basketball. When players miss, they are assigned a letter. Players are out when they accumulate all the letters in the word.
2. Player 1 serves to a zone.
3. Player 2 serves next and must serve to the same zone.
4. If player 2 misses the zone, player 2 receives an H.
5. If player 2 hits the zone, player 2 serves to a zone that player 1 must hit next or risk receiving a letter.

Coaching Point

Make your servers spell out something unique to your school or team.

Variations

- Require players to jump-serve.
- Increase the number of players per group.

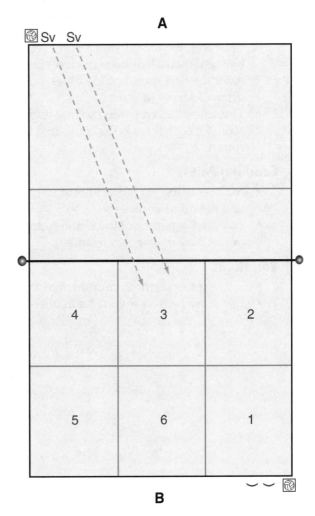

QUADS SERVE AND PASS

Purpose

To encourage aggressive and accurate serving and to improve accuracy of serve reception.

Setup

Players are divided into teams of four, labeled groups 1, 2, 3, and so on. The number of teams does not matter. Group 1 is on side A serving to group 2, which is passing on side B. Group 3 on side B serves to group 4, which is passing on side A. A cart of balls is on each endline for the servers. A target from the passing and shagging teams is in zone 6 on both sides at the net.

Run the Drill

1. Every team will serve at least one round and receive at least one round.
2. Each group of servers serves 25 balls each round. The serving team gains a point for each ace served.
3. The first three missed serves do not count as points for the receiving team, but all missed serves after the third one do. One server counts the number of service attempts for the team; another server counts all the aces.
4. The receiving team gains a point for every ball that is passed and caught by the target. They keep track of the number of passes caught.
5. After the first round of 25 serves, teams switch: Group 2 serves to 1, and group 4 serves to 3.
6. The sequence is repeated so that each group plays every other group. The score for each team is the combined total of its serving round and passing round.

Coaching Points

- Make sure the players are accurately counting the number of balls served and the number of aces.
- You can keep track of the winners and run a tournament during the week or just play one or two rounds.

Variations

- Run a tournament in round-robin format.
- Use more passers if your team does so in competition.

Sv
Sv
Sv
Sv

A

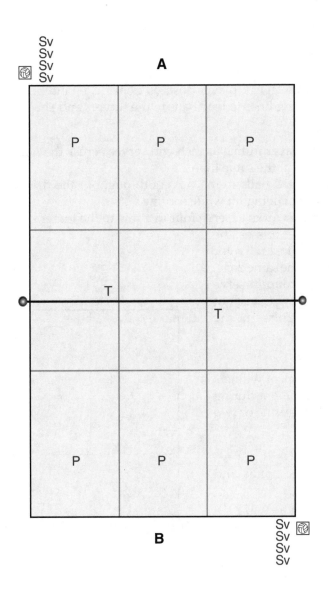

B

Sv
Sv
Sv
Sv

Purpose

To encourage accuracy and consistency in a competitive setting.

Setup

A group of four servers sets up on each endline. Cones or tape mark the three back zones on the court: player-position zones 1, 6, and 5. Extra players set up near the serving lines to feed balls to the servers and shag the served balls.

Run the Drill

1. The first player in line at each end serves across the net to zone 1. Both sides serve at the same time.
2. Shaggers feed balls to the servers throughout the drill and protect the servers from being hit while serving.
3. Each group works to serve four in a row to the target zone.
4. If one server misses, the team must start over serving to the same zone.
5. The first group to serve four in a row to each of the three zones is the winner.

Coaching Point

You can keep track of winners and run a tournament during a week or just play one or two rounds.

Variations

- Change the zones and groups.
- Beginners can try to get the ball in the court rather than in a specified zone.
- Advanced players can serve to all six zones.

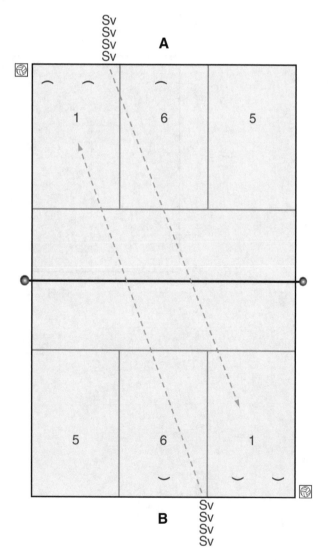

Purpose

To encourage strong serving against two or three passers and give players a competitive opportunity to complete the rally.

Setup

Two groups of three, preassigned or not, spread out across each endline. A basket of balls is at each endline. The first groups of three from each side begin on the court.

Run the Drill

1. One player from side A serves the ball. If the result is an ace, then side A receives 3 points and the teams on both sides are replaced.
2. If the ball is served out, the group on side A leaves the court and is replaced, but the team on side B stays on, and side B has scored 1 point.
3. If the ball is served into play and is passed, a rally ensues, and players compete 3v3 until the ball is dead. The winners of the rally receive 1 point for their side, and both teams are replaced.
4. Side A must score 9 points before side B scores 7.
5. The game is short. After the first contest, the sides can play again with side B serving to see which side earns the most points. Play two out of three or three out of five with the same sides.

Coaching Points

- Teams get to play all the groups on the opposing side because when a serve is missed, the receiving side stays and the serving team is replaced.
- Giving bonus points for an ace encourages servers to be more aggressive.

Variation

Assign specific players who need serving practice to serve an entire game while the other players just play triples.

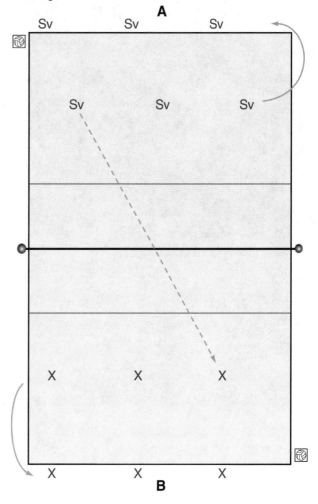

chapter 3

Ball-Handling Drills

Passing drills are quite often a player's first introduction to the game of volleyball. Although, arguably, the serve is as important (You can't win if you can't serve, as the saying goes), the pass is used more often than any other skill in the game.

Handling the ball well starts with good body position. The player should be in a medium stance with knees bent, legs slightly more than shoulder-width apart, and the right foot slightly forward.

Players can pass received balls with a forearm pass or an overhead pass. Make sure that players are using good form for both types of passing before they perform these skills in drills. Make corrections and adjustments during and after drills as needed.

Use these training cues to help your players master forearm passing:

Beat the ball.

Contact the ball on the forearms away from body.

Platform, or create the passing surface, to the target.

An overhead pass differs slightly from a set (a ball that is directed overhead directly to a hitter for an attempt at termination) in that the passer must absorb the impact of a ball coming with pace. To absorb that impact, the passer should round the shoulders forward, lower the hands to face level but under the eyes, and tighten the core muscles as the fingers contact the ball.

Use these training cues to help your players master overhead passing:

Beat the ball.

Shape the ball at the forehead or higher.

Square to the target.

Extend as needed.

Passes can be ranked, or scored, as 3, 2, 1, or 0. Assuming that the pass is being made to a target (the setter), a 3 pass is one that gives the setter three options in which to set: The pass is accurate and the setter has the option of setting any one of the three hitters at the net. A 2 pass is one that makes the setter move a bit, causing the setter to have only two options at the net. A 1 pass is one in which the setter moves quite a bit and can set the ball to only one option. A 0 is a pass that gives no options to the setter.

It is a good idea while developing the pass as a skill to begin to record scores at practices. Players can call their own passes. For example, a player executes 15 forearm or overhead passes to a target from a tossed or served ball and calls 3, 2, 1, or 0 after each pass. A partner can total them. Divide the score by 15 to get the passer's average pass score. An average of 2.3 indicates a fine passer, and a score of 1.0 indicates a weak passer. Knowing their passing scores shows passers where they have room for improvement and gives them a goal. It is useful to record passing scores in drills and in matches.

> **If you don't focus on passing drills early in the season, you *will* be focusing on them the rest of the season.**

When deciding which passing drills to run, consider players' strengths and weaknesses as passers and their level of experience. Monitor their skills as the season progresses and provide additional challenges. Early on, basic serve-receive drills allow players to see and read the ball as well as to practice calling the ball and getting behind it. As players improve, they are ready for drills that require passing with more pace and accuracy. The goal is to prepare them to perform at a level that will allow them to be competitive with the opposition they will face. Be sure that players have a chance to handle the type of serves they will face in competition; if necessary, the team's stronger servers or coaches can stand in for the opposition.

All passers need numerous repetitions. One-on-one passing, repetitive passing drills, and small-group passing games allow for many touches and should be done extensively early in the season. Cooperative drills in which players aim for a certain number of tasks completed are effective, but be sure to add a competitive scoring system as soon as players are ready.

Beginners need to experience more coach-centered drills early for instructional purposes. More advanced players can run player-centered drills. Advance to combination drills that use two or more skills within a drill as soon as the passing is at a level that allows this. All players will receive more gamelike passing experience in multiplayer drills and team drills throughout the season. While the midseason and postseason offer less opportunity for individual drills, it is fine to add a technical drill for a checkup once in a while. If the skill level is dropping, a quick review and repetitions are often what are needed.

A player's presentation of self when preparing for a pass is important. Using consistent, correct form every time can eliminate error. This includes the ready position. Players whose presentation establishes that they want the ball to come to them can be intimidating to the opponent. A strong presentation also encourages passers to feel confident and in control. Tell players to *look big*!

Purpose

To improve the percentage of successful passes.

Setup

The drill can be run concurrently on both sides of net. Three passers and one setter set up on each side of the net. A coach or tosser and a basket of balls are stationed off court on the opposite side of the net from the passers. The coach sets the clock or timer to three minutes.

Run the Drill

1. The coach throws or enters the ball to the passers across the net.
2. A passer calls the ball and passes it to the setter, who announces the number of points awarded for the pass: 3 is a pass to the setter at shoulder height or above with no movement on the part of the setter; 2 is a pass within two steps of the setter; 1 is a pass in which the setter can chase down the pass and still act; 0 is an overpass or ace in which the setter has no chance to act on the ball.
3. The setter catches the ball and throws it back to the shagger stationed near the basket.
4. Play continues on both sides for the allotted time. Players try to pass for as many points as possible. The side with the most points wins the round.
5. New groups enter or the same teams can play two out of three or three out of five.

Coaching Points

- Encourage lofted passes but not *sky* balls. This encourages a faster-paced game.
- Enter balls at a consistent pace to the passers. Try not to speed up near the end of the drill in order to help a team score more points.

Variations

- Have a play-off in which primary passers (those who pass the most balls) compete against primary passers, secondary passers (those who sometimes pass) against secondary passers, and third-line passers (those who rarely or never pass) against third-line passers.
- Add a hitter and set the ball to them, but keep the focus on the passers.

A

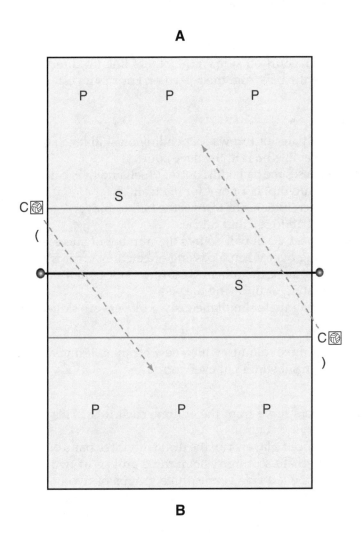

B

CONTROL PASSING

Purpose

To master control of the forearm and overhead passes.

Setup

Players are divided into teams of two. One player from each pair lines up with a ball in the back court on side A; the others line up directly across the net, ready to receive the ball from their partner. Four pairs can be on the court at the same time.

Run the Drill

1. Player 1 initiates or throws (depending on skill level) the ball across the net to player 2, who is in the deep court.
2. Player 2 passes the ball with control to self and then catches the ball. Each successful attempt is a point for the team.
3. Player 2 then initiates or throws the ball to player 1 across the net, who passes the ball to self and catches.
4. Players repeat. Each pair counts the number of successful attempts in a row, starting over when a passing or catching error is made. Each team competes against the others. Teams are not penalized for errors made while initiating or throwing the ball.
5. Teams can compete simultaneously if players are skilled enough.

Coaching Point

Run the drill for three minutes with a new group entering after the time limit is up, or switch in substitutes at every error.

Variations

- Have players serve from the endline each time. This allows players to practice serving control.
- Have advanced players run the drill with three pairs of players per team. Use an alternate scoring system: three groups of two work together as a team on the left side versus three groups of two on the right side. In this variation, two players are on the court at a time. Each pair gets two attempts to score three in a row, and then a new duo takes their place. Count total sets of 3 points scored per team.

A

B

Purpose

To give liberos the opportunity to compete head to head using the serve and pass.

Setup

A line is marked down the middle of both sides of the court with tape, cones, or other markers, and a basket of balls is on each endline. Libero 1 sets up to serve on side A. Libero 2 sets up in position 5 on side B to receive. A coach sets up in position 6 at the net on side B with an empty ball cart.

Run the Drill

1. Libero 1 serves to libero 2, who passes to the coach.
2. The coach catches and rates the pass on a 0-to-3 scale, based on the number of options available for setting.
3. If the pass is a 3, libero 1 serves again. Each libero attempts to pass as many 3 passes in a row as possible.
4. When libero 2 passes something other than a 3, libero 2 serves from his or her side of the court and libero 1 has the opportunity to receive and score points by passing 3s.
5. Two missed serves in a row scores a point for the passer. A ball served to the opposite side of the court from the passer is considered a missed serve.
6. The first libero to score 11 wins.

Coaching Point

Watch players carefully. This is a great opportunity to determine which libero handles pressure better.

Variation

Add a primary passer who passes with both liberos so that they are challenged to work together.

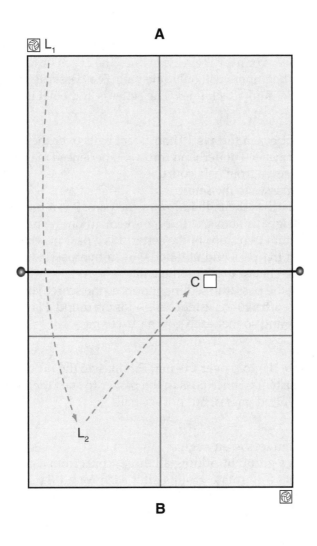

Purpose

To increase passing accuracy.

Setup

A tosser or coach with a ball, a passer, and a target (setter) get into position on each side of the net at or near the service line. The coach or tosser should have a basket of balls. Beginners use only one ball. The passer is in ready position between the service and attack lines. The setter is at the net in zone 6.

Run the Drill

1. The tosser or coach throws 10 consistent balls over the net to the passer. Beginners may need underhand throws; experienced players may advance to a simple serve from half-court.
2. The passer passes to the setter.
3. The setter catches the ball and rates the pass: 3 is a pass to the setter at shoulder height or above with no movement on the part of the setter; 2 is a pass within two steps of the setter; 1 is a pass in which the setter can chase down the pass and still act; 0 is an overpass or ace in which the setter has no chance to act on the ball.
4. After rating the pass, the setter announces the score. The passer with the highest score after 10 consistent balls wins the round. Players switch places after each round so that each gets a turn to pass.

Coaching Points

- Demonstrate the toss over the net. Emphasize the need for the tosser to send a consistent bounce pass to the passer to start the drill.
- Encourage lofted passes, but not *sky* balls.

Variations

- The tosser can toss at an angle.
- Compete as a group by adding all three scores from a group.
- Play as teams and rotate groups after each round (i.e., all of the tossers play with each other against the passers and targets).
- Repeat with the same group to try to beat a previous score.
- Establish a high score that all teams try to beat in subsequent practices.

A

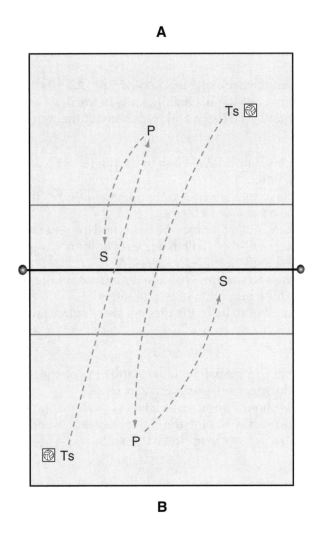

B

Because this drill is more gamelike than the often-seen three-person pepper, it is an effective warm-up drill.

Purpose

To use a gamelike ball-control drill as a means of warming up.

Setup

The court is split lengthwise using markers or tape. A setter and hitter begin at the net on side A and on side B. One digger is in the deep court with another digger directly behind. The coach and feeder are off the court near the net.

Run the Drill

1. Initiate the play with a tossed ball to the digger, who passes to the setter, who sets the hitter.
2. The hitter hits or makes a one- or two-handed throw (if necessary) to the digger on the other side of the net.
3. At this point, the hitter becomes the setter, and the setter becomes the hitter. They alternate with every ball that goes over the net, moving behind each other after the dig—not side by side.
4. Players attempt to sustain a continual sequence of dig, set, and hit with four players for a minimum of two minutes.
5. After a set number of balls, the diggers switch places with the hitter and setter.

Coaching Points

- Have beginners tip the ball with one hand or push the ball over with two hands at the digger until proficiency increases.
- Hitting skills should improve as players perform the skill more often. Have players practice tossing the ball to themselves and hitting it against the wall or to a partner to improve the skill.

Variation

Have players change from offense to defense without stopping play of the ball by move quickly right after the ball is hit over the net. This is a fun challenge. Walk through the transition a few times for beginners until it becomes natural.

A

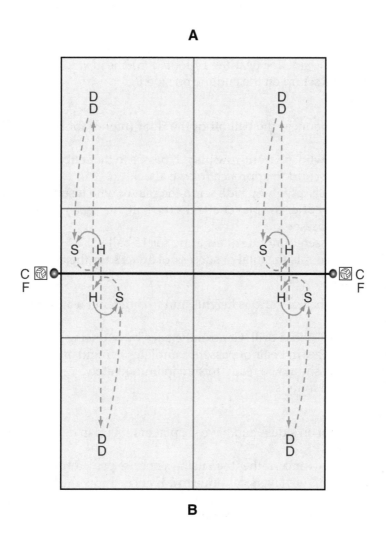

B

Purpose

To improve efficiency in movement pattern from passing to hitting.

Setup

A coach, a team of two passers, and a setter get into position on side A. The coach sets up at the sideline near the 10-foot (3 m) line next to a feeder and cart of balls. Shaggers set up on the endline on side B.

Run the Drill

1. The coach bounces the ball off of the floor (higher for beginners) to the passer.
2. The passer, who is a front-row player, passes to the setter and then transitions off the court to approach for the attack.
3. The setter sets a high-outside set to the player who just passed the ball.
4. Immediately after the player attacks the ball, the coach bounces a ball to the second passer.
5. The two passers continue alternating for 12 balls.
6. The coach counts the total of successful attacks for the team.

Coaching Points

- Bounce the ball to various heights and to different areas as players progress.
- This is a fast-paced drill. Control the pace by bouncing quickly.
- As soon as the first pair of passers completes a round of 12 balls, the next two players should be ready to step in immediately.
- Play several rounds.

Variations

- Run the drill on side A and have six players set up in defensive positions on side B.
- As players advance, rather than using a bounce pass, throw or toss the ball to the passer. As players continue to advance, throw the ball over the net to the passer. Finally, you or another player can serve the ball to the passer.
- Put a coach, passers, and a setter on each side of the net. Players should hit the ball down the line.

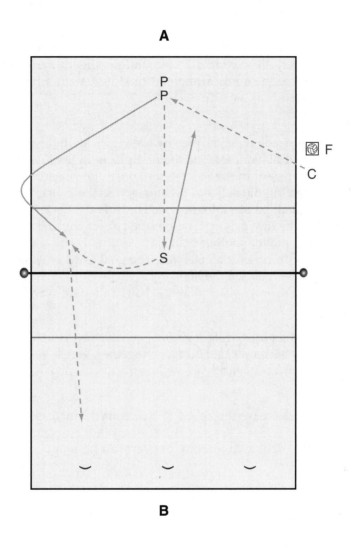

Purpose

To increase the amount of time players can maintain focus while passing

Setup

Six to eight players spread out along each sideline, facing one another. They should be staggered slightly rather than standing directly across the court from each other. One coach stands at the end of side A with a basket of 60 balls. Another coach stands at the side B endline.

Run the Drill

1. The coach on side A begins play by tossing a ball to the first player in one line, and that player passes to the first player in the line across the court.
2. That player passes the ball across the court, and play continues with each player receiving the ball and passing across the court. The last player to receive the ball passes it to the coach on side B.
3. As soon as the first player passes the ball down the line, the coach on side A tosses the player another ball.
4. Repeat this process for all 60 balls. The goal is for players to pass all the balls all the way down the line.
5. When a ball drops, collect all of the balls and start over.

Coaching Points

- This is a tremendous drill for giving players many contacts in a short time.
- As players communicate and work together, watch leaders emerge and position them strategically in the line the next time you run the drill.

Variations

- Increase or decrease the speed of ball entry to increase or decrease difficulty.
- Perform this drill with forearm or overhead passing.

A

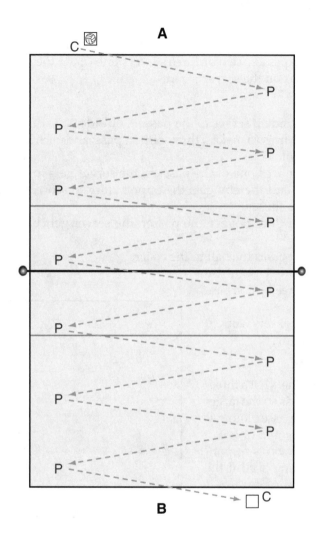

B

Purpose

To encourage players to serve aggressively and to make a three-option pass.

Setup

Three passers get into position on side A. The coach sets up near the net to act as a target for the passer. Two or three servers line up on the endline of side B. A basket of balls is on the server's end.

Run the Drill

1. A server on side B serves to the passers on side A.
2. Each passer tries to make a three-option pass, and each server tries to ace the opponent.
3. If the server aces one of the passers, the server gets to take the place of that passer and thereby gets the opportunity to score, while the passer becomes the server.
4. If the server does not ace the passer, the server gets back in the line to serve.
5. The passer passes the ball to the coach.
6. Passers score 1 point by passing a three-option pass to the target.
7. As a team, passers work to score 10 points

Coaching Points

- Predetermine what a three-option pass is so the target can let the passer know if the passer scored or not.
- Determine who is responsible for being aced if the ball is between passers.

Variations

- Increase or decrease the number of points needed to win the game.
- Delete a point for a missed serve or for two missed serves in a row.

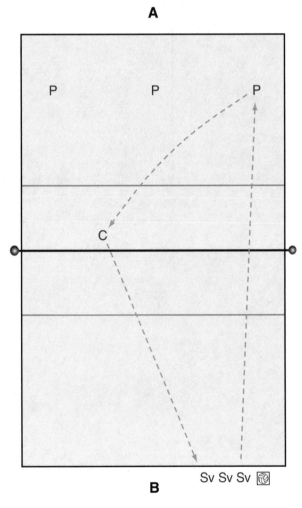

LONG-COURT PEPPER CHALLENGE

Purpose

To train hitters to dig, transition, and approach while attacking with control.

Setup

Move the antenna to the center of the net to create two long courts. Two players set up on side A, one at the net and one in the backcourt. Two players set up on side B, one at the net and one in the backcourt.

Run the Drill

1. A player on side A tosses the ball over the net to side B to initiate the drill.
2. Players on side B pass, set, and attack the ball.
3. Players on side A pass, set, and attack the ball.
4. This continues until the number of cooperative attacks over the net reaches 12.
5. When an error occurs, the players switch positions.

Coaching Points

- Adjust the number of contacts to suit the skill level of the players.
- Consider players' abilities when assigning roles as setters or hitters.

Variations

- Have the player at the net block so that the backcourt player reading the hitter is in a more gamelike situation.
- Increase or decrease the number of successful attacks according to your team's level.
- Make the players switch positions each time the ball goes over the net.
- Younger or less experienced players can tip, set, or roll-shot the ball over the net.

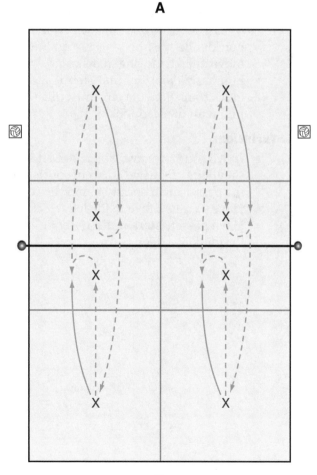

Purpose

To improve agility when passing and to practice transitioning quickly and beating the ball to the spot.

Setup

Four tossers set up at the net on side A and side B. Each tosser has a ball. Four passers set up on each side of the net on the endline, facing the tossers.

Run the Drill

1. Tossers toss the ball in front of the passers.
2. Passers pass the ball back to the tosser and then move to the right in a counterclockwise manner as they transition back to the endline.
3. Tossers toss the ball again and the cycle repeats.
4. Once a passer gets to the sideline, the passer passes the ball and then sprints to the other side of the net.
5. After the passers go through all tossers four times, the passers and tossers switch positions and go again.

Coaching Points

- Make sure passers move their feet to the ball. They will have a tendency to pass and move at the same time. Teach them to pass, then run back quickly. Besides helping to condition players, this encourages them to move quickly during matches.
- Emphasize that the first step is most critical when transitioning. For a quick transition, players must push forward off the back foot rather than pull with the lead foot.

Variations

- If two courts are available, have all eight tossers and eight passers on the same side of the two adjacent courts. When the passer gets to the sideline, the passer must sprint behind the courts back to the far-left position.
- Have passers move to the left (clockwise).
- Have passers start at the 10-foot (3 m) line and transition to the endline to simulate a deep ball.

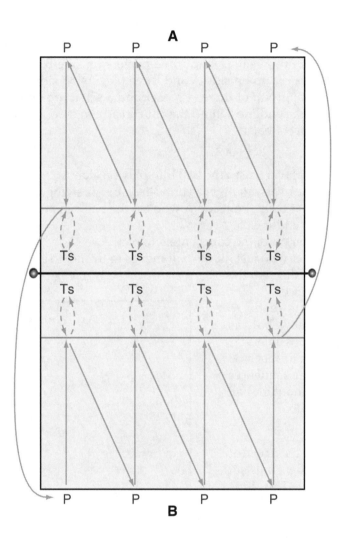

Purpose

To work on ball control in a gamelike manner.

Setup

An antenna is used to split the court down the middle, creating two courts. Three players set up on side A and three players on side B of court 1 on the left. Three players set up on side A and three players on side B of court 2 on the right. For each group of three, a passer and a setter are on the court, and one player is on the endline behind the court ready to enter. A coach is on the sideline with a cart of balls.

Run the Drill

1. A coach or player tosses the ball into play on side A.
2. Side A passes, sets, and hits a controlled shot or swing to side B.
3. The player at the net on side A who set the ball runs to the endline and touches the endline.
   - The player off of the court enters to pass.
   - The player who just hit the ball moves to the net to set the next ball.
4. Side B goes through the same sequence.
5. The coach is ready to toss in a new ball as quickly as possible.
6. The goal is to reach 30 pass, set, hit sequences in a row without the ball hitting the floor.

Coaching Points

- If the teams are not reaching the goal, set a time limit. This adds urgency to the drill.
- Use this drill to help the less experienced players learn the game. Provide direction as needed.

Variations

- Dictate what type of shot must be made: roll, tip, two-handed set, back-row attack, or 50-percent swing.
- Increase or decrease the number of sequences required.

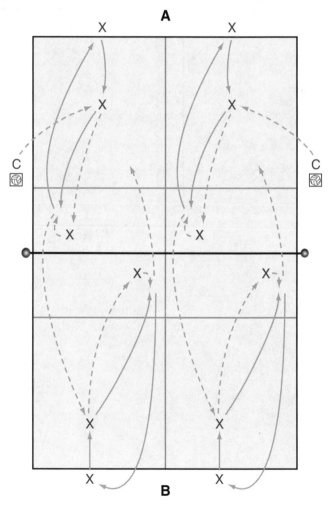

Purpose

To provide a large number of passing repetitions of controlled ball handling.

Setup

Two passers set up on side A and two on side B. Two players set up at the net as catchers in positions 3 and 6 on side A and on side B. Each catcher has a ball. The coach puts three minutes on the clock.

Run the Drill

1. Each catcher tosses the ball across the net to the passer on the opposite side.
2. After tossing, the catcher immediately catches the ball from the passer on his or her side of the net and again throws the ball to the passer on the opposite side of the net.
3. Players try to pass 20 passes to the target within the three-minute period.

Coaching Points

- Remind players to catch the ball on their own side of the net and to throw across the net to the opposite side.
- Encourage players to be aware. It is the responsibility of each of the four players who are throwing to avoid hitting the other ball coming in from across the net.

Variations

- Put an additional passer in each line.
- Run the drill for time instead of a number of repetitions.

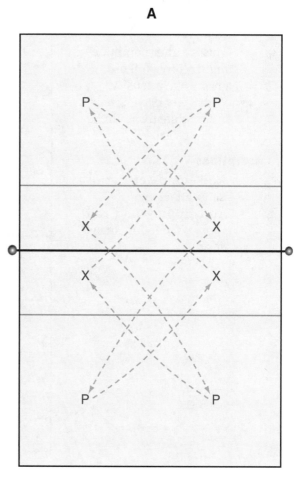

Purpose

To allow players to warm up and work on conditioning while practicing all aspects of ball handling.

Setup

Six to eight pairs of players are on the court. One player from each pair lines up near one sideline; that player's partner lines up near the opposite sideline. Coaches set up around the court with carts of balls. The coach puts 30 seconds on the clock and starts the drill.

Run the Drill

1. Partners begin to pepper: By turns, they set, attack, dig, set, attack, dig, and so on.
2. After 30 seconds, the players on one sideline rotate clockwise to face a new partner. The player in the bottom position moves up to the top.
3. The coach puts 30 seconds on the clock to give players time to switch positions and starts the drill again.

Coaching Points

- Emphasize proper arm swing.
- This is a great conditioning drill for defense, so encourage intensity.
- With fewer players, have them rotate through the group twice.

Variations

- Add jump-setting or jump-attacking.
- Add tipping and roll shots as needed or as desired.

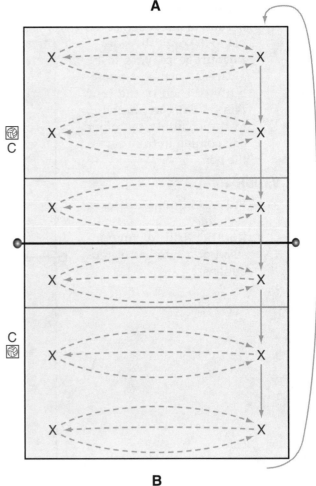

PASS OUT

Purpose
To promote efficient ball handling and court movement.

Setup
Three players set up in a row on side A. A coach is off the court on side B with a basket of balls.

Run the Drill
1. The coach enters a free ball to player 1 on side A.
2. Player 1 passes the ball to player 2, and then player 1 immediately runs to side B.
3. Player 2 sets the ball to player 3, and then player 2 immediately runs to side B.
4. Player 3 hits the ball to one of the players on side B and immediately runs to side B.
5. Players continue to pass, set, and hit, changing sides five times.

Coaching Points
- Insist on fast movement from side A to side B.
- Discuss with players how the situation and location of other players determine where the pass should go.

Variations
- After a group crosses over the net five times, change which players are the passer, setter, and hitter.
- Increase the amount of times necessary to cross the net to be successful.

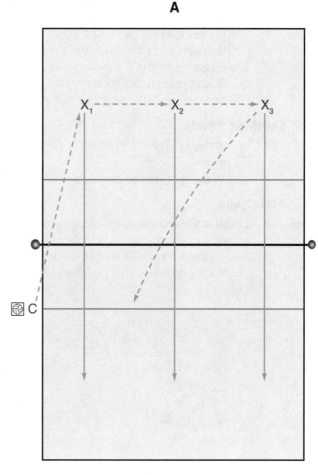

Purpose

To pass successfully while performing multiple tasks of passing, covering, and relocating.

Setup

Three passers set up on side A, and one passer waits behind the endline ready to be the next passer. Four servers are on side B, with one positioned as a target to catch the pass on side A and the others are at the endline with a supply of balls. The coach puts three minutes on the clock. The coach designates a set that the passers must cover after the pass.

Run the Drill

1. The coach starts the clock.
2. The first server on side B serves the ball to side A.
3. A passer on side A passes the ball to the target. Once the pass is made, the passer moves to the net to cover the designated set.
4. The two remaining passers shift to a different position.
5. The player from behind the endline enters the court and joins the other two passers in the open position.
6. The player that just served the ball transitions to a designated defensive position and then becomes the target on side A.
7. The target from the previous pass catches the ball and then runs back to side B and gets in line to serve.
8. The coach counts the number of 3 passes made within the three minutes.

Coaching Points

- Encourage players to get used to the outside disruptions and focus on the pass.
- Remind players to communicate with one another as they perform the drill.

Variations

- Count a missed serve as a 3 pass for the passing side.
- Increase or decrease the number of passes required to win the drill.
- Assign the servers zones in which to serve.
- Place your middles in a position to pass short balls.

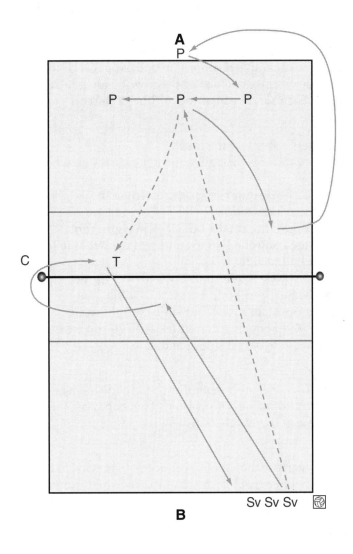

Purpose

To improve ball control, encourage communication, and minimize hitting errors.

Setup

Setters are in the right-front position on side A and side B throughout the drill. Players set up in the other five positions on both side A and side B. Substitutions enter into right back immediately after their own team attacks the ball over the net. A coach is on each sideline near the middle of the court with a cart of balls.

Run the Drill

1. Coach 1 enters a free ball to side A.
2. Side A passes and sets the ball to the left-side hitter, who hits a controlled ball to side B.
   - Once the left-side hitter sends the ball over the net, side A rotates clockwise to the next position.
   - The setter does not rotate, but stays in right front.
3. Side B digs the controlled attack and sets the left-side hitter, who attacks a controlled ball to side A.
   - Once the left-side hitter sends the ball over the net, side B rotates clockwise to the next position.
   - The setter does not rotate, but stays in right front.
4. This cooperative sequence continues until 20 successful attacks and digs have been made between side A and side B.

Coaching Points

- Be patient. This drill takes repetition before the team becomes successful.
- Allow players to play each position. This enhances their understanding of the game and their ball-control skills.

Variations

- Increase or decrease the number of successes needed to complete the drill. If the players have trouble meeting the required number of attacks and digs, put a time limit on the drill.
- Position the setter in the middle front so that the setter sets both left front and right front.

A

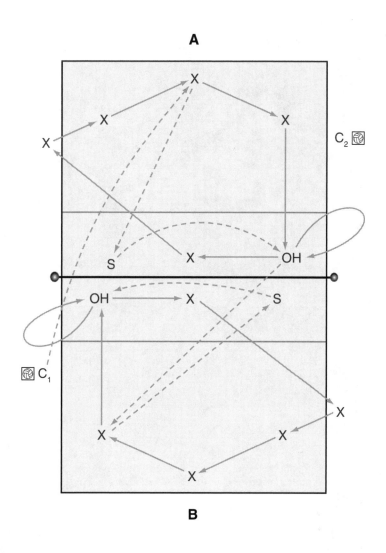

B

Setting Drills

Setters are responsible for feeding the ball to the offensive players for termination. Setters can also terminate the ball themselves. A successful setter typically performs numerous repetitions daily and often sets extra balls before and after the rest of the team is finished practicing.

During preseason, it is critical for setters to work on technique and repetitions in private sessions. Hitters can be added to these sessions when setters are ready, but the emphasis must be on set accuracy from various positions on the court.

Getting to the ball is as important as the actual set. Setters need repeated training in preparatory movement. Establish a medium height (knees slightly bent), with the intent to run to the place on the court where the pass is sent and the set will occur. It is almost as if the setter at the net were in starting blocks ready to explode before a race.

Use these training cues to help players master setting:

Beat the ball.

Shape the ball above the forehead.

Square to the target.

Extend as needed.

A quicker, lower set ball does not need complete extension of the arms, but a ball set high to the outside calls for full extension.

The attitude and behavior of the setter in drills generally reflects the team's attitude and behavior during drills. Talk to the setter independently of the rest of the team. Share expectations constantly so that the setter knows what is expected. Input from the setter is valuable. Typically, the setter becomes an extension of the coach on the court.

It is imperative to drill every type of set within an offensive system. If setters first perform numerous repetitions without hitters, they perform more efficiently in repetitions with hitters.

The most common drill for individual setting repetitions is the triangle drill. Player can set several of the same type of sets in a row before changing to another type. All sets used in match play should be drilled.

Include repetitions that require explosive movement to the net. The setter must be able to quickly move into position. Drill sets that involve transition work between them, such as movement to the net, movement to the ball, and movement to defense.

A setter who plays front row must also work on offensive attacks, including the hit and dump. Having an offensive-minded setter is nearly equivalent to having an extra attacker, with the added element of surprise!

Be sure to include repetitions from dug balls as well as set balls. Address setting from various locations: frontcourt and backcourt and even chased off court. Practicing tough setting situations prepares the setter to handle those situations during competition.

With the exception of technique work, most setting drills can be run at a quick pace. A quick pace in practice prepares the setter for a quick pace in match play. To keeps things moving and still incorporate feedback from coaches and hitters on the set, use a common system of communication. The comments must be concise and must be called immediately after a set in repetitions drills. Here are some commonly used terms:

Tight: a ball set too close to the net

Off: a ball set too far away from the net

Deep: a ball set past (farther than) the intended attacker

Short: a ball set not quite to the intended attacker

High: a ball set above the intended height

Low: a ball set below the intended height

Using these simple feedback words (alone or in combination, such as "high and tight") can minimize the time used to explain a set, making practice more efficient. Using an established vocabulary also ensures that the remarks are interpreted as critiques rather than criticism. All players should have knowledge of these feedback terms and be able to use them when working with a setter. It is important to give positive feedback when a set is on the target. A simple yes is generally understood as positive feedback.

Within an offense, each set is given a name or a number so that players know what to expect. The set is identified by its height, trajectory, and placement along the net.

Develop a series of zones along the net that works for your team's level. Establish which zone the setter will use as the target area. Typically, if a team uses a nine-zone system along the net, the setter sets from zone 5. If a team uses a seven-zone system, the setter sets from zone 6. A young beginning team might have three zones, one for each front-row player.

It is not necessary to run the same number of sets as the national team. They are elite, and most teams cannot handle an offense that complicated. The number of zones along the net does not matter. What matters is that your team knows the system.

The high set to an outside hitter might be a 5 for one team and a 4 for another. Many teams name the set by combining the zone number with the height of the ball. For example, a set that is three feet high to zone 3 would be a 33 or shortened to a 3. It might be called gold on another team for its school color. It is important to name sets at the net and in the backcourt so that there is a common term for each set in a system.

Allow and encourage setters to play to win! The setter who is instructed to set everyone equally in practice will likely do so in matches. If all players truly understand their roles on the court, then it is no secret that everyone on the court does not hit equally. It does not usually work well to set every ball to one hitter because deception is part of the game, but top hitters should get more swings in drills and in matches.

Tactical development begins when we start adding combinations to drills. For example, a coach might ask a setter to make an explosive move to a position, set the ball to an attacker who is likely to score, and oh, by the way, while doing this, listen for the set the hitter is calling for and watch the blockers' positions on the opposite side of the net so that the correct hitter is chosen. Providing opportunities in drills for setters to develop gamelike transitional skills and decision-making skills sets them up for success on match day.

Because the setter must be prepared to send the ball in either direction, this drill reinforces the importance of receiving the ball at the same location above the forehead. It also adds a mental aspect to a physical repetition drill.

Purpose

To practice adjusting to last-minute directions to set the ball.

Setup

A setter gets into position at the net in zone 6 on side A. The coach stands in the middle back with a basket of balls on side A. Targets are in zones 1 and 9 with the empty ball carts.

Run the Drill

1. The coach tosses a ball to the setter positioned in zone 6 at the net.
2. The coach calls out "front" or "back" before the ball reaches the setter.
3. The setter either sets a front 4 or a back 9, depending on the call.
4. The setter tries to set 24 balls in the correct direction.

Coaching Point

As the setter improves, delay the call to challenge the setter.

Variations

- Add a live passer.
- Replace the call with a middle blocker who makes a step in one direction so that the setter must set in the opposite direction.

A

This is a basic but critical drill. Players sprint to the net 24 times—8 from right back, 8 from middle back, and 8 from left front (zones 1, 6, and 4 respectively)— and set 24 outside sets (4s).

Purpose

To improve footwork to the net out of the serve-receive patterns and improve the consistency of the sets.

Setup

A coach sets up on side A in the middle-back area with a basket of balls and a feeder. Setter 1 is in the right back with setter 2 behind her or him. Setter 3 is in the left front ready to catch the set.

Run the Drill

1. The coach tosses the ball to setter 1, who has sprinted to the net and is *setter ready* in zone 6 along the net.
2. Setter 1 sets the 4 ball, covers, and becomes the next catcher.
3. Setter 3 catches setter 1's set and sprints to the coach, hands the ball to the coach, and sprints to the end of the line to set.
4. Setter 2 runs to the net to set after setter 1 has completed her or his set.
5. Each setter sets eight times from the right back, then the group of setters moves to the middle back for eight repetitions each. The group then moves to the left front for eight repetitions each.

Coaching Points

- Insist on a full-out sprint to the net on each repetition.
- Give feedback on the consistency of each set.

Variations

- Change the locations for where the setter starts.
- Alter the type of sets the setter will perform.

A

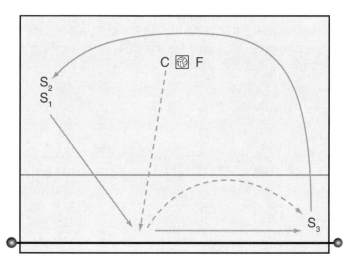

Players try to set as many successful balls as they can in each round, with the ultimate goal of performing 100 to 1,000 sets, as ability allows.

Purpose

To improve accuracy of sets through repetition.

Setup

A coach or tosser, a setter, and target players in the hitter position set up on one side of the net. Another setter or two can line up on the sideline, ready to replace the setter. Balls and a feeder are next to the tosser (alternatively, a rapid-fire, two-ball system can be used). The coach gives the setter the designated sets before initiating play.

Run the Drill

1. The tosser tosses the ball to the setter at a consistent height for each series.
2. The setter sets the assigned set to the target in the hitter position.
3. Players repeat the sequence with the same setter for at least 5 sets; 10 is best. It is better for setters to perform more repetitions in a short time than to perform only a few repetitions and then wait for another turn.
4. The next setter in line steps up to take a turn without breaking the rhythm. The transition is quick.
5. At least two rounds are completed before changing to a different set.

Coaching Points

- This is a rapid-fire drill—be quick.
- Three or more players can perform this drill every day before or after practice.
- Use all sets in this drill. Don't neglect the right-side sets.

Variations

- You can set up another triangle on the opposite side of the net.
- The toss can come from various positions on and off the court.
- Make the setter jump-set all balls.
- Have the setter start at various positions away from and along the net.
- Make the setter move to the ball to replicate a pass off the net. You may have to use one setter at a time for a series of two or three when making the setter move.

A

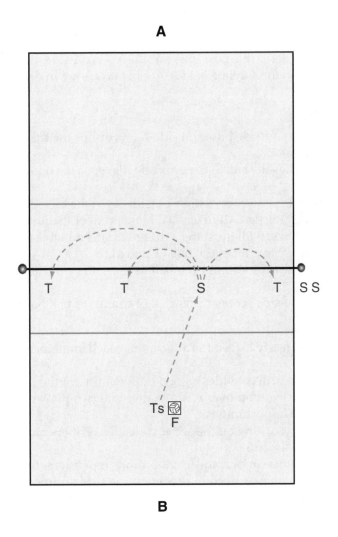

T   T   S   T S S

Ts
F

B

Purpose

To give the setter the opportunity to dig, transition, cover the hitter, and finally to transition to set the outside hitter.

Setup

Six players are in defensive positions on side A. An outside hitter or coach with a cart of balls is on the sideline of side A. Six players are in defensive positions on side B.

Run the Drill

1. The coach or outside hitter on side A hits or tips the first ball at the setter on the same side.
2. The setter digs the ball to the opposite player as the outside transitions to attack.
3. The opposite player sets a high-outside set to the outside hitter or a set to the middle attacker. All defensive players cover the hitter.
4. The rally plays, with the setter setting all balls possible after the first ball.
5. Setters alternate after every one or two plays.
6. The coach always initiates the ball at the setter on side A after the rally has ended.
7. The winning side scores 1 point; play continues to 8 points.

Coaching Points

- Have a ball ready to feed the attacker or coach immediately after the rally ends.
- Because this drill provides a good opportunity for the opposite player to practice setting, you may wish to alternate two players in that position to share the opportunities.
- Focus your coaching on the setter transition. Hitters must also transition quickly in this drill.
- It is sometimes important to give more repetitions to one setter over another, so you may need to predetermine a substitution ratio or routine. For example, you could give the starting setter three plays and the second setter two plays, maintaining that sequence throughout the drill.

Variation

Initiate play with a toss over the net to side B, who must pass, set, and attack the setter in the right-back position on side A. This adds a specific dimension for side B, but keeps focus on the setter transition on side A.

A

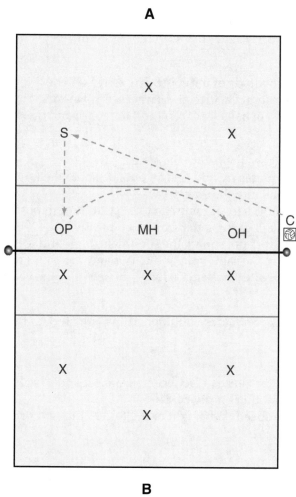

B

This is a fantastic drill to start the setter training session because it reinforces proper technique.

Purpose

To give the setter the opportunity to square the shoulders, hips, and feet to the target. To develop consistency in the set regardless of where the pass comes from.

Setup

Players set up on one side of the court. The setter is in position 6 at the net. The coach begins in position 1 at the net. A target sets up in zone 4 with an empty cart. A feeder with a cart of balls sets up behind the coach and moves with the coach.

Run the Drill

1. The coach tosses the ball to the setter.
2. The setter squares up and sets an outside set to the target in zone 4, who places the ball into the empty cart.
3. The coach moves in an umbrella (arc) pattern from position 1 to position 9, tossing a ball to the setter from each position.
4. If the setter does not square the shoulders, hips, and feet to the target, the coach stays at the same spot and tosses another ball. The coach moves to the next spot after the setter squares up and sets the ball properly.

Coaching Point

Make sure the setter squares shoulders, hips, and feet to the left side of the antenna.

Variations

- Have the setter alternate between a front set and a back set. Add another target and another empty cart.
- Increase the speed and height of the toss as the setter progresses.
- Add a passer.

A

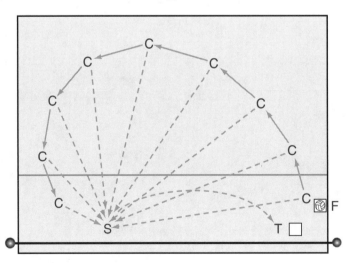

SALT-AND-PEPPER SETTING

In this drill the setter has a chance to get in 200 quick repetitions, 100 front sets and 100 back sets, off a live pass.

Purpose

To improve the consistency of the set.

Setup

This drill is run on one side of the court. One setter is in zone 6 at the net. A passer is in the middle back. Coach 1 is in zone 1 at the net with a ball. Coach 2 is in zone 9 at the net with a ball.

Run the Drill

1. Coaches alternate tossing to the passer, who passes the ball to the setter.
2. The setter alternates setting the front set and the back set.
3. When coach 1 in zone 1 tosses the ball, the setter should back-set that ball.
4. When coach 2 in zone 9 tosses the ball, the setter should front-set that ball.

Coaching Point

Provide consistent feedback to the setter.

Variations

- Make the passer move with the toss so that the pass may be more difficult to set.
- Hit the ball to the passer to simulate dug balls.
- Position players in zones 1 and 9 and have them set the ball back to the passer. Use just one ball.

A

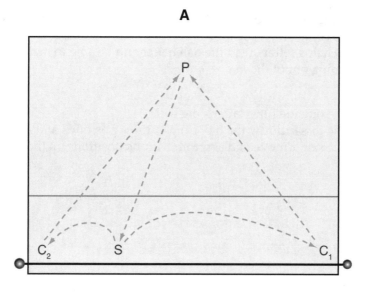

HIGH–LOW, OUT-OF-THE-NET SETTING

Purpose

To give the setter the opportunity to retrieve balls out of the net and set them to a hitter without panicking.

Setup

Setters are at the net in a single line. A target is in the outside-hitter position with an empty basket. A coach or tosser sets up in the middle of the court with a supply of balls. Space exists between the active setter and the other setters.

Run the Drill

1. The coach throws the ball into the net, consistently throwing the ball to the lower half of the net.
2. The setter attempts to set the ball by staying low. The setter should try to set the ball with the hands if possible but can use the forearms if necessary.
3. The target catches the ball and puts it in the basket.
4. The next setter in line takes a turn, and the action is repeated for several rounds.
5. The coach then throws the ball at the top half of the net, and the sequence is repeated.
6. Finally, the coach mixes high and low tosses, and each setter sets three balls per turn. The goal is for the setters to set two or three balls in a row to the target.

Coaching Points

- Point out to players that balls that go to the bottom half of the net, or go in low, tend to come out high. Balls that go into the top half of the net, or go in high, tend to come out low.
- Encourage players to see that the speed of the ball is a factor in how the ball will come out of the net.
- Practice helps setters read the ball better and be able to make a play on a ball coming out of the net.

Variations

- Have the outside hitter attack the ball.
- Have the tosser throw the ball from various positions and angles.
- Have the setter move and set from various positions on the court.

A

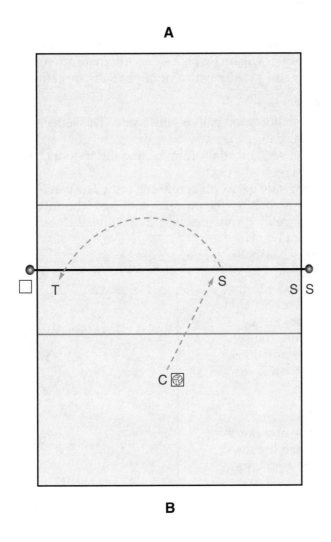

B

Purpose

To encourage the setter to chase and set every ball.

Setup

Three back-row players set up on each side. Substitutes are on the endline behind each player. One setter will set for both sides. Alternate setters wait at the side of the court. A tosser and a feeder with a supply of balls are at the side of the court.

Run the Drill

1. The tosser initiates the ball to either side. The setter moves to the side receiving the ball as the ball is tossed.
2. Players pass, set, and attack from behind the 10-foot (3 m) attacking line. The setter stays at the net.
3. The winning side gets a point for each rally. The game is played to 8.
4. The substitute behind the on-court attacker who just attacked the ball switches places with the attacker. Switching is done on the run, even during the rally.
5. Each setter sets 10 balls, and then the next setter in line comes onto the court. However, the rally must come to an end before the setters change positions, unlike the back-row substitution.

Coaching Point

Encourage your attackers to call the set using the designations your team has established.

Variations

- Have setters alternate every rally.
- Attackers can stay on court until they commit an error on any skill. The endline player behind the player who committed the error then takes a turn on the court.
- Place a setter on either side.

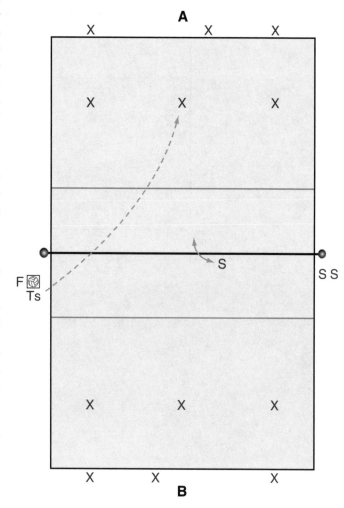

DUMP TRUCK

Purpose

To improve confidence, technique, and accuracy in a variety of dumps by the setter or opposite player.

Setup

The drill can be run on one or both sides of the net. Three or fewer setters or opposites are used at a time. One coach sets up on the same side of the net as the setter or opposites. Shaggers are on both sides. A basket or shagger is on the court in each of three target areas: deep line, crosscourt, and reverse.

Run the Drill

1. The coach tosses the ball to zone 6, starting with high and tight tosses for easier dumping.
2. The setter jumps into the setting position as if to set, and then extends the left arm high and dumps the ball to the target.
3. Each setter dumps two balls to each target and then moves to the end of the setting line.
4. Players score points by dumping the ball to designated target areas. The coach counts the number of dumps that score per round or team. Players try to beat that number the next time through.

Coaching Point

Keep the action moving at a fast pace. Remember that many repetitions in a short time are more beneficial than repetitions spread over a longer period.

Variations

- Have one setter dump to a given target seven times. Then setter 2 performs the same action trying to beat setter 1's number at the same target. Repeat for all the setters or opposites, changing targets every two rounds.
- Play against a team of six and add a hitter to the setter's side. This gives the setter the option to set or dump and keeps the defense honest.

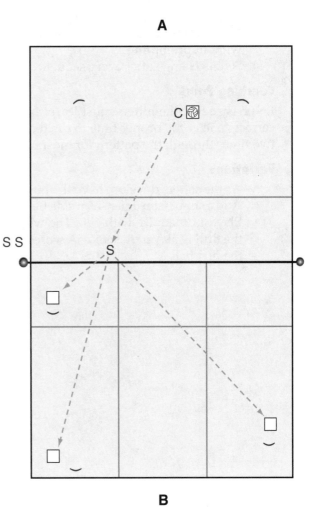

This is a great way to pit setter against setter.

Purpose

To develop consistency when performing a variety of sets.

Setup

Before practice, the coach prepares two to four pattern cards, listing a series of 15 sets to be done in a given order. Three hitters (targets) and a setter take their places on side A. Alternate setters wait off court. A coach or tosser is at midcourt on side A with a feeder or two and a supply of balls. Shaggers set up on the sideline near an empty cart.

Run the Drill

1. The setter and hitters on the court quickly review the sets, then hand the card to the alternate setters.
2. One setter sets the entire pattern of 15 sets (or dumps) in a row.
3. Hitters must take a full approach, catch the ball, and roll the ball off court to a shagger, who places the ball in the cart. The alternate setter should help call out the sets at the beginning of the drill. As the setters and hitters learn the sequence, players should run the sequence with better pace and without prompting.
4. Setters change after every sequence.

Coaching Point

Emphasize that the hitters must learn the pattern also so that they are in the correct zone at the proper time to catch or attack the ball. It only takes one or two times through the pattern for most players to learn it.

Variations

- As the setters develop, have the hitters attack the ball.
- Add a six-person defense on side B and only let side A know the sequence.
- Play out the rally with 6v6. The winner of the rally scores 1 point, and the drill is played to 9. Side A scores 2 points instead of 1 if they score on the first ball.

A

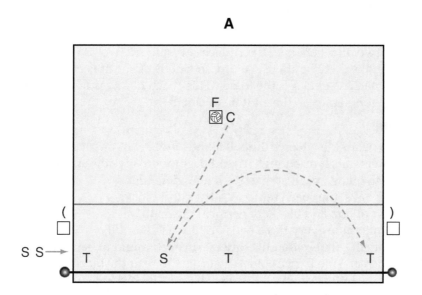

Purpose

To give setters the opportunity to practice isolating a hitter by reading the opposing blockers.

Setup

A setter and two attackers take their places on side A. Two or three blockers, depending on the attack options, set up on side B. A coach is on each side of the net. The coach on side A is the tosser. This coach has a feeder and a supply of balls. Shaggers set up on the endline of side B.

Run the Drill

1. The coach on side A tosses the ball to the setter, who can set either attacker. The setter waits long enough to read the block to give the attacker the best chance to hit against just one or even no defender.
2. After 12 balls, the coach replaces hitters and blockers.
3. The new hitters and blockers perform the drill.
4. Setters alternate every three balls or after each round.
5. Alternate the attacks that the hitters run each round or each ball.
6. The coach on side B gives blocking orders to read the block or to commit on specific hitters or on all hitters. The middle blocker changes on each set. The next middle at the 10-foot (3 m) line behind the blocking middle is ready to replace the blocking middle.
7. The goal is for the attackers to score on as many attacks as they can out of 12.

Coaching Points

- Predetermine all sets and attacks to be used.
- Assign someone to count successful attacks each round.
- Focus on helping the setter see (read) the blockers and tendencies of the blockers.

Variations

- Add a full defense to side B.
- Have the setter also dump the ball.
- Create a competition between groups of setters and hitters for each round.

A

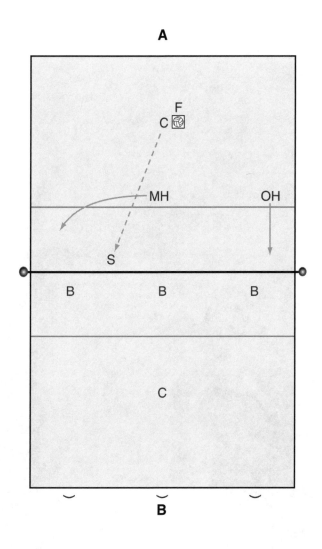

B

chapter 5

Offensive Drills

The attack is the attempt to terminate the ball over the net into the opponent's court. Most crowds go crazy over a beautiful swing above the net that results in a booming blow to the opponent's side. It is one of the high points of volleyball. The offensive attack might be the most complex skill in volleyball because of the movement that must be performed while timing the set ball and establishing the hitting shoulder behind the ball.

The attack involves taking a three- or four-step approach to the set ball, taking off from one foot or both feet from a planted position, and jumping high behind the set ball to hit (or tip or roll) the ball, usually with an open hand, into the opponent's court. Because the skill is a complex blend of movements and timing, the attack is often broken into parts. Players often improve through repetitive drills that emphasize one aspect per session, slowly advancing until they are ready to put the parts together and focus on the attack as a whole. This whole, part, whole approach can be used with other offensive skills as well if necessary.

You can't change everything in an attack at once. It's a long process. Sometimes it's best to simplify the individual attack and just tell players to "run and hit!"

However, it's possible to get too caught up in the details. Although it's important to emphasize a sound approach, good shoulder position, an explosive takeoff, and a fast arm swing, focusing too much on the individual components can lead to a robotic, strained attack. Players also need a chance to learn by doing and to develop a feel for the skill.

Don't forget left-handers when teaching the attack. While a three-step approach for a right-handed attacker is left, right, jump; a left-handed attack is right, left, jump. A right-handed attacker uses a wide left-to-right angled approach. A left-handed attacker uses a wide right-to-left angled approach.

Use these training cues to help players master the attack:

Take a running approach.

Explode from heel to toe.

Contact in front of the hitting shoulder.

Follow through.

Land on both feet.

The offensive game, even at lower levels, has advanced in complexity in recent years. Even younger teams are running fast-tempo offenses, especially in the middle of the court. To coach an offense with a wide variety of attack options—possibly including high, quick, shoot, slide, pump, and more—many repetitions of every type of attack and in every zone in which each attack will be used are necessary. Do not shy away from letting young players experience the joy of different attacks. We often find that some attackers actually attack a quick-set ball with more efficiency than a high set. The timing of the high set often gives beginners difficulty.

Fast athletes like to run the offense fast. The team's ability to create different offensive tempos depends on the quality of the pass, dig, and set, but running offensive drills increases the team's chance of success. The speed of an offense is based on the speed of the athletes and the level of ball control. In other words, the better the ball control, the quicker the tempo.

Once players have reached a level of success with their individual repetitions, it is time to introduce combination plays. The left-side hitter might hit a high set, the middle hitter a quick set, and the right-side player a slide set. In serve-receive drills, the setter usually indicates by hand signals which hit each player might receive. Attackers should all be of the mindset that they *will* receive the set. The middle attacker approaches quickly for a quick set, taking off before the set. If the middle attacker does not get to set the ball, this jump serves as a fake to the opponents.

Many combinations can be run in the course of a match, so players must be well prepared. The following drills offer practice in running team offense as well as opportunities to get in lots of repetitions in an exciting manner. Many of the drills use competition to raise the level of enjoyment and add a gamelike flair to practices. Remember, Coach, an attack that succeeds is a point on the board—every time.

Purpose

To improve scoring ability on the first-ball attempt against six defenders.

Setup

Six players set up in defensive positions on side A. A passer, setter, and hitter get into position on side B. Another group of three waits at the endline of side B. Each side should include a passer, setter, and hitter (in any attack position). A coach stands off of the court on side A with a supply of balls. A player, manager, or assistant coach keeps score for side A.

Run the Drill

1. The coach enters the ball to the passer of the group on side B.
2. That threesome attempts to pass, set, and terminate the ball. If they succeed, they receive a point and get to stay.
3. If side A is able to block the ball or is able to pass and set the ball, then side A receives a point. A partial block, pass, and set also score. Players can sub into side A.
4. The group of three on side B stays on until it does not score, alternating play with the group behind the endline.
5. Play continues until the first threesome gets 5 points or the defense has 15 wins. After a game, two new groups enter on side B or the winner stays against a new opponent.

Coaching Point

Encourage players to make quick transitions on group changes.

Variations

- The winning side of the net can choose offense or defense for the next drill.
- Pit middle attacker against middle attacker. Be sure to use all attacking positions.

A

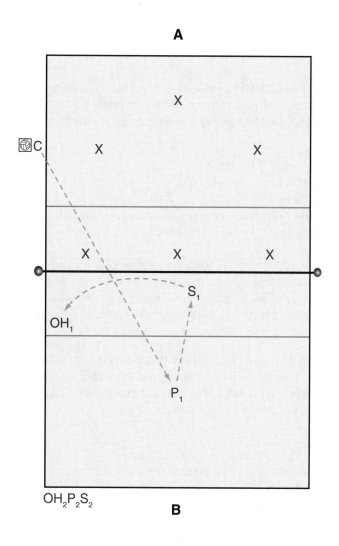

OH₂P₂S₂

B

This is a great repetition hitting drill. Players try to score as many points as possible in the minute allotted.

Purpose

To improve the percentage of attacked balls that score.

Setup

The coach or tosser has a basket of balls at midcourt. The setter is in position at the net. Three hitters line up on the sideline. The clock is set to 60 seconds, and the counter is ready. Shaggers set up on the opposite side of the court.

Run the Drill

1. The coach tosses to the setter.
2. The setter sets a high-outside ball.
3. The hitter attacks.
4. As soon as the hitter hits, the coach sends another ball to the setter, who sets it to the same location. The hitters alternate using the same attack position.
5. The hitters score 1 point for an in-court attack. Beginners can score a half-point for a successful tip or roll shot.
6. Each hitter counts the number of points scored in one minute.
7. The next group of hitters sets up and takes a turn.

Coaching Points

- Be consistent. Have middle hitters compete against middle hitters with the same set or opposites against opposites with the same set.
- Keep the action fast paced. Have the next group ready to go with no break.
- Repeat for all positions with a variety of sets.

Variations

- Narrow the target section of the court.
- Have outside hitters compete against middle hitters.
- Allow players to call their set. But for consistency, practice and repeat the same choice for the entire minute.
- Begin with three hitters on the court, one in each attack position for one minute: OH-MH-OP vs. OH-MH-OP. Establish sets before starting.

A

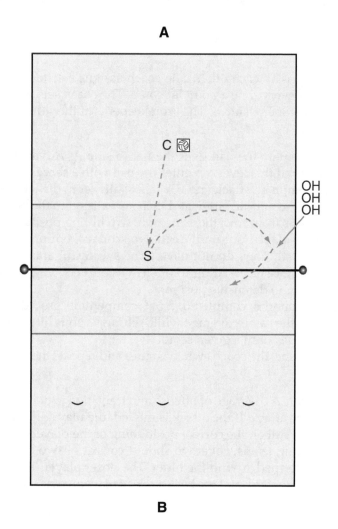

B

Purpose

To learn to cover all areas surrounding the attack in case the ball is blocked back into the courtside and to transition to defensive positions if the ball is not blocked.

Setup

Two teams of six play each other. The coach assigns a schedule for subbing, which will occur every time a point is scored. The coach sets up with a supply of balls at the sideline of side B. The scorekeeper is at the sideline.

Run the Drill

1. The coach enters the ball over the net to side A. Advanced teams who have mastered this level can enter the ball with a serve.
2. Side A attempts to attack and cover six balls set to the left-side hitter, six balls set to the middle hitter, and then six balls set to the right-side hitter. If the setter is front row, there are only two hitting positions.
3. Each ball is played out until dead. No score is kept until the 18 attacks are completed. They do not have to be successful attacks. Emphasis is on correcting issues relating to offensive court coverage by players and transitioning to defensive positions.
4. Once this round is completed, a 6v6 competition provides opportunity to work on the same coverage while setting various hitters in game play. Play continues until a given score.
5. After the game, the coach switches sides and repeats the drill with side B.

Coaching Points

- Focus on side A coverage of offense and transition to defense only. Do not focus on the attack. If the attack is missed, the play still counts and your emphasis is still on the correct positioning of the players.
- For beginning teams, coverage should consist of two concentric circles of players formed around the hitter. The closer players are there for balls blocked downward, and the back circle of players covers the deep blocked balls.
- You may run this drill without balls, covering each hitter a few times until players are comfortable with where to go and how to transition back to defense. Add balls when you feel players are ready.
- This is an instructional drill to correct errors and improve on transition. It is not rapid fire.

Variations

- Run this drill without balls one day, with balls but without scoring the second day, and with balls and scoring the third day. Transition takes time.
- Deduct points if the team scores but does not cover the attacker.

A

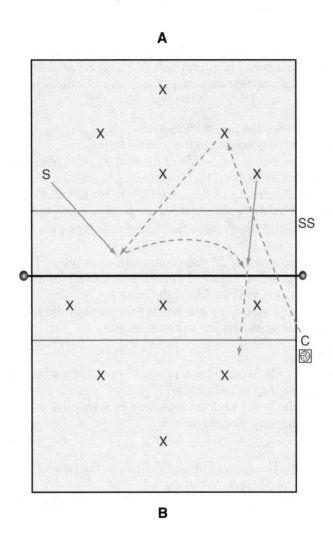

B

Purpose

To practice hitting angles with intent from a middle quick attack.

Setup

A coach or tosser with a supply of balls sets up on side A at midcourt. Three middle hitters and a setter begin on side A. Shaggers or defensive players set up on side B. Baskets or markers are in the center of side B.

Run the Drill

1. The coach tosses the ball to the setter.
2. The setter sets a quick set to the middle hitter.
3. The hitter hits crosscourt, wide of the baskets or markers. The hitter goes to the end of the line and the next hitter takes a turn.
4. Hitters must alternate angles, attacking to the left and then to the right.
5. The setter should encourage these angles by setting the ball on (straight up) or off (slightly past the hitter, forcing the hitter to turn in the air and hit crosscourt).
6. One round consists of 12 tosses, four attacks per hitter. The goal is to score as many as possible out of 12 attempts. A successful attempt is one that is hit in the court but outside of the markers.
7. The drill is repeated with a different group of middle hitters or repeated with the same group trying to better its score.

Coaching Points

- During the drill, have hitters practice repetitions of each angle before alternating swings to each angle.
- Make sure the setter understands the job of helping the hitter make the angles by properly placing the set.

Variations

- Add a passer. The tosser initiates the ball to the passer.
- Add defensive players on side B.
- Instead of alternating left and right angles, let the setter and hitter determine the angles.

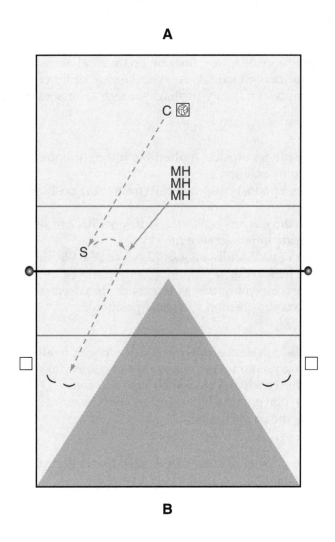

Purpose

To give outside hitters the opportunity to transition and attack the ball from different angles on the court.

Setup

One group of three outside hitters lines up on the sideline next to the left-front outside hitting position on side A. A second group of hitters spreads out on side B with an empty cart, ready to shag. A coach or tosser sets up on side A with a basket of balls.

Run the Drill

1. The outside hitters on side A alternate hitting the tossed ball from the coach into court-position 2.
2. The coach continuously tosses 25 balls from court-position 2 to the outside hitters.
3. If more than three errors occur, the score goes back to zero and the group of three outside hitters starts over.
4. Once group 1 successfully attacks 22 out of 25 balls, the group switches and group 2 gets to hit.
5. The same process continues as the coach or tosser moves from court-position 2 to court-position 1 to court-position 5.

Coaching Points

- Toss the balls high so that the hitters learn to wait to attack the ball.
- As the tossing point moves from corner to corner, make sure the hitters open up to the coach and close their hips and core.
- Discuss with players which parts of the court are easier to attack according to where the ball is tossed.

Variations

- Decrease the number of successes needed to complete the drill.
- Count a ball that touches the tape as an error.

A

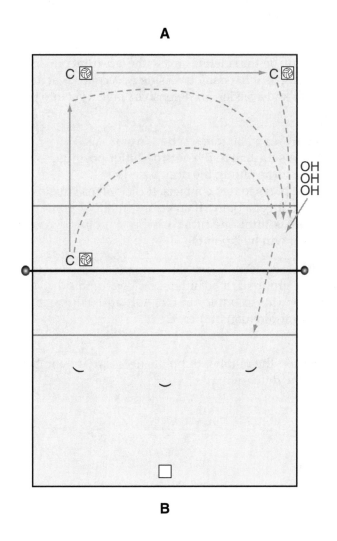

OH
OH
OH

B

Purpose

To give hitters in the same position the opportunity to compete head to head and learn the value of every attack.

Setup

Three hitters line up on the sideline next to the left-front outside hitting position on side A. A setter gets into position on side A. A coach is at midcourt on side A with a cart of balls and a feeder. Six defensive players get into position on side B.

Run the Drill

1. The coach tosses a ball to the setter on side A.
2. The setter sets the ball to the outside-hitter position.
3. Hitters take turns hitting the designated set.
4. The defense plays to two contacts. If the defense makes two touches, the hitter does not get a point. If an error is made, 1 point is deducted.
5. Play continues until one hitter reaches 5 points through terminations. Hitters must win by 2 points.

Coaching Point

You can have any group of three hitters compete in this drill either by position or by combination (for example, an OH, OP, and MFB against each other or against another combination of three).

Variation

Increase or decrease the number of points necessary to win based on the level of the hitters or the defense.

A

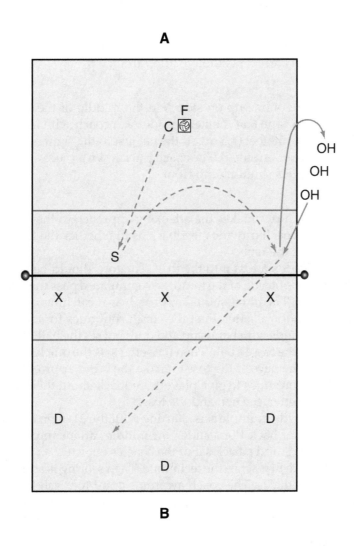

B

Marking the spot to jump from gives hitters a visual cue that keeps them from being too tight to the net or setter.

Purpose

To give the middle hitters the opportunity to attack three different sets while teaching them the correct position to jump from.

Setup

Three middle hitters line up on side A in the middle of the court. A setter is ready to step into zone 6 at the net on side A. A coach with a cart of balls sets up on side A about 15 feet (4.5 m) off the net just to the right of the middle line. Shaggers spread out on side B. The coach puts down a piece of floor tape at the position the middles should jump from.

Run the Drill

1. The middle hitter makes the attacking approach to the net at 50 percent speed. The coach provides feedback as to whether the feet were in front of or behind the tape.
2. The coach adds a toss into the drill. The toss should be a high ball from behind the right side of the middles to simulate a pass the hitter must wait on to attack. The hitter should approach as if catching up to the ball.
3. The coach adds a setter. First the coach continues tossing the ball while the setter stands with hands up and does not set the ball; the middle hitter still attacks the tossed ball. Then the setter sets the quick attack. The coach speeds up the pace of the toss to make the hitter approach more quickly.
4. The coach continues to give players feedback about their spacing in relation to the setter, the net, and the toss.
5. The coach adds multiple sets, starting with the 31, then adding the 1, and then a tight or back 1 or a slide. The middles attack three balls in succession: a 31, a 1, and a back set of the coach's choice.
6. At first, the drill teaches the technique. Then scoring is added for the three successive attacks. The coach awards 1 point for each kill that does not hit the tape and deducts a point for an error (a ball that goes out or hits the tape). The player with the most points after five times through wins.

Coaching Points

- Provide constant feedback during this drill.
- Have a second coach watch the hitters' spacing and whether or not they are open to their setters.

Variation

Add a live passer and toss from over the net.

A

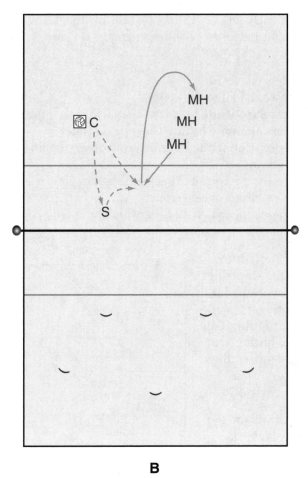

B

Purpose

To provide the opportunity to hit aggressively while eliminating hitting errors.

Setup

An outside hitter sets up in the left front prepared to attack. Another hitter waits at the sideline. A coach sets up 15 feet (4.5 m) off the net with a cart of balls and a feeder. A setter gets into position in zone 6 on side A. Shaggers spread out on side B.

Run the Drill

1. The coach tosses a ball to the setter.
2. The setter sets the outside hitter, who attacks down the line.
3. The two hitters alternate hitting the outside sets.
4. Each hitter tries to attack 10 balls in a row down the line without making two errors in a row.
5. If a player misses the zone but keeps the ball in play, it is a wash and does not count as an attack or an error.
6. The sequence is repeated with hitters attacking crosscourt.

Coaching Points

- Emphasize the follow-through to the opposite hip when players are hitting line shots.
- Emphasize dropping the thumb of the hitting arm when players are hitting crosscourt.

Variations

- Put a time limit on the drill to help players learn to hit aggressively when the pressure is on.
- Add a passer or have the outsides pass to themselves.
- Run the drill with two right sides or two middle hitters.

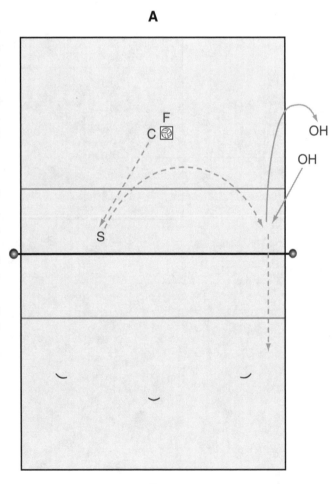

Purpose

To give one player the opportunity to hit a variety of attacks repeatedly.

Setup

On each side of the net a coach or tosser with a basket of balls, a setter, and two attackers get into position. The coach assigns three sets to each set of hitters.

Run the Drill

1. The coaches toss the ball, the setters set, and the first hitter in each line attacks.
2. This is repeated two more times to the same hitter.
3. The second hitter attacks the same three sets.
4. Every clean attack in the court earns 1 point. A ball that is tipped or rolled is a free repeat. Only one repeat per round is allowed.
5. Repeat for three rounds. The player who scores the most points is the winner.

Coaching Point

Make sure that the hitter is explosive on every approach, whether hitting with power or executing an off-speed attack.

Variations

- Middle hitters can compete at the same time if they move out of the middle to the left.
- Two attackers can compete against each other on opposite sides of the net. This can be done individually with one attack throughout the round or with three to five different attacks within one round.
- Add a passer and have the coach or tosser toss the ball over the net to the passer, who sends it to the setter.

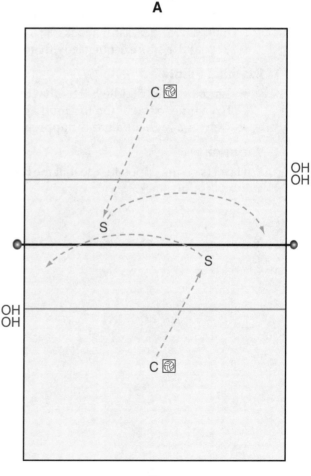

⚐⚐⚐ ONE STEP, TWO STEP, THREE STEP

Purpose

To enable the middle hitters to attack effectively when they can transition only a short distance before hitting.

Setup

A middle hitter is at the net on side A in a blocking stance. A coach sets up in zone 6 at the net on side A with a basket of balls and a feeder. Shaggers set up on side B.

Run the Drill

1. The coach tosses a ball to the middle hitter.
2. The hitter transitions one step off the net and attacks the ball.
3. Play continues until the hitter has made five successful attacks.
4. The sequence is repeated, but in this round the middle hitter transitions two steps off the net to attack the ball. Play continues until the hitter makes five successful attacks.
5. The sequence is repeated, but in this round the middle hitter transitions three steps off the net to attack the ball. Play continues until the hitter makes five successful attacks.
6. Repeat the entire sequence with another hitter.

Coaching Points

- Emphasize to middle hitters that they can be effective even if they don't have time to transition for a full approach.
- Deliver a higher ball as the approach increases in distance.

Variation

Put targets on the opposite side that the hitter must hit for the ball to be counted as a successful attack.

A

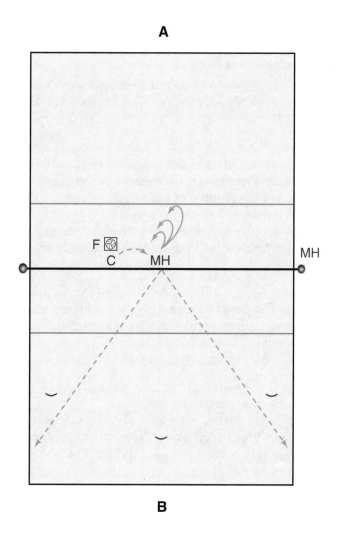

B

This drill gives players the confidence to use a variety of attacks in a game.

Purpose

To give hitters and setters the opportunity to run a variety of attacks in a given order.

Setup

On side A, an outside hitter, a middle hitter, an opposite, and a setter take their positions. A coach or tosser with a supply of balls sets up at midcourt. Shaggers spread out on side B.

Run the Drill

1. The coach provides hitters with a sequence of 12 to 14 attacks to perform. Players can take a few minutes to review the sequence.
2. The coach tosses the number of balls in the sequence. Players set and hit according to the sequence.
3. After going through a sequence a few times, the coach starts to keep score. The hitting group receives 1 point for every cleanly attacked ball hit into the court.

Coaching Points

- Keep the drill fast paced! Encourage players to transition quickly.
- Run the same sequence with various setters and have them compete against each other.

Variations

- Add a passer. The tosser then initiates the ball from the opposite side of the net, and the passer passes to the setter.
- Add a defender on the opposite side, keeping up a fast pace.
- Use one or two different sequences in one practice. Do not overload players' minds by using more than two. It is better to perform several repetitions of two sequences than to do two repetitions of several sequences.

A

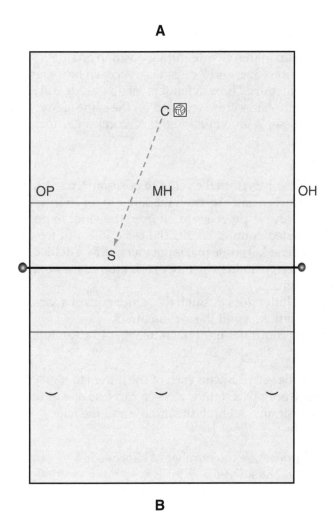

B

Purpose

To give an attacker the opportunity to transition from one attack to a second attack and then a third attack.

Setup

Three hitters line up in the outside-hitting position on side A. Three setters start at the net in positions 3, 6, and 7 on side A. A coach or tosser with a supply of balls sets up at midcourt. Three defenders set up on side B at right back, middle back, and left back. A tosser is stationed on the same side for each setter with a basket to the tosser's immediate right. A scorekeeper for each hitter counts the number of kills.

Run the Drill

1. The first hitter hits from the setter in position 3, transitions, and immediately approaches and hits from the setter in position 6, then immediately transitions, and approaches to hit from the setter in position 7.
2. The designated counter counts the clean kills out loud as the drill progresses. A clean kill is one that is not touched by a defender. After attacking from all three positions, the hitter runs around the court and gets back in the hitting line.
3. The second hitter goes through the same series of attacks, starting as soon as the first hitter has hit the second attack.
4. The process continues until the hitters get 15 clean kills.

Coaching Points

- Designate the set you want each of the hitters to hit.
- If you have only two setters, a coach can toss one of the sets or have the setter in position 6 set both the middle and the back.

Variations

- Increase or decrease the number of kills needed.
- Alter what is considered a kill.

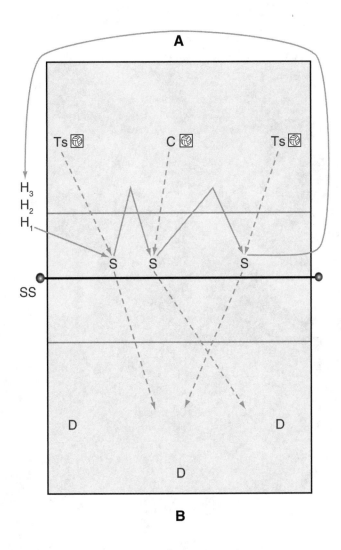

chapter 6

Defensive Drills

You've probably heard of or referred to teams as being scrappy on defense. If you brand your team defense with quickness and early preparation and reading on the court, it shows during matches. A strong scrappy defense can actually wear out some strong offensive teams, either by fatiguing them or frustrating them.

Whenever the opponent has the ball and you are defending or protecting against their attack, you are said to be on defense. This includes the block, which is the first line of defense, and the dig, which is the second line although not less important. Every player has an area of the court to protect and each is responsible for acknowledging which attacker on the opposing side will likely attack.

Blockers establish ready position, with the forearms in front of the body, approximately a forearm's distance from the net, prepared to jump or move left or right. Eyes are up. Generally, they see the pass, watch the set to judge where it is going and assess its trajectory, find the hitter, move, and block. Sound easy? Not at all!

Timing is crucial for a good block. The blocker usually takes off a split second after the attacker takes off. How much bend in the knees the blocker should have before the takeoff depends on the strength of the jumper, but it should not be greater than 90 degrees. A strong core is necessary for a strong block. *Hang time* is what a blocker dreams of, how long the blocker can maintain the block position on the opponent.

Coaching players to block well requires guiding them through a progression of steps: blocking instruction, blocking without a ball, blocking with a ball, movement to block without a ball, movement to block with a ball, and the total blocking action. Drills should build the skill. Some players may struggle to successfully block because of lack of height. Some can soft-block—block with wrists bent back so as to guide the ball to a second-line defensive player to dig. (Remember that a blocked ball that remains on your side of the net does not count as a contact, so the dig is considered the first contact.)

Use these training cues to help players master the block:

Run.

Explode.

Sneak in; sneak out.

Land softly.

Blocking drills need to start early in preseason so players can advance progressively. When coaches attack at beginning blockers, it is important to hit *at* their hands so that blockers experience the feeling of success when starting. It is equally important when adding balls, to give them practice in following the pass, tracking the set, and then seeing the hitter. Many players don't automatically do this, and you might find them waiting and waiting and never seeing a ball at their area of the net. That player is then no help on either first- or second-line defense.

When running to double-block, players use a crossover step (or run). The blocker turns to the direction of the set and then runs, breaks, and blocks. A shorter distance might require just a simple hop-step. Drills should incorporate both types of movement in repetition and in many multiplayer and team drills so players get enough opportunities to read, move, and block with efficiency. Remember, a stuff block (which scores directly) is a point on the board!

Digging is the second line of defense. If the blockers read well and set a good solid block, then that "wall" takes out an area of the court to defend, thus the second-line diggers can cover outside the area that's already protected. Individual digging drills call for a great deal of repetition, but this book offers many varieties of drills with competitive opportunities for players to dig.

Digging is done in a low position, with legs wide and weight distributed evenly but slightly forward. The digger must always be aware of the court boundaries and keep the ball in front of the body whenever possible. As soon as the attacker is ready to hit, the digger should have both feet on the ground and be leaning forward. The digger uses the platform (forearms) to push through under the ball, creating backspin so that the ball will go up. Defensive players ideally should stay on their feet, which makes the transition to cover easier.

Use these training cues to help players master the dig:

Get a platform behind the ball.

Shift weight forward.

Push through the ball to the target.

Defense demands that players react to the offensive move. A player blocks or digs where the ball is hit, and until then, the player does not know where to go.

All defensive players have the responsibility of communicating where the set is going and where the hitter is aligned when attacking (down the line or at an angle). If the attacker tips or rolls, it should be called. The defensive player who can read how the play is developing on the opposite side of the net has a big advantage. That player will be prepared before the attack.

Players should call the ball and then transition to coverage. Once the block or dig is made, the team is immediately on offense. Teams must practice this quick transition repeatedly in drills.

> The plan should always be to outwork the opponent in the back row. It makes a noticeable difference.

When a team is doing an effective job of covering the court defensively, the actions of the players have a flow that appears effortless at times. It seems that just six people easily cover the entire area.

You can choose from different types of defenses, depending on the experience, speed, and ability of your team, but the choice also depends on the offenses that are played against you. Where do the opponents hit from? What is their pace of play? What tempos do they use in their offensive attack? Are there numerous free balls? A simple good defense is much stronger than a fancy defense that players either can't grasp or can't run.

Focus on individual defensive skills early in the preseason. Advance to combination plays after that. Finally, put players together for small-group play. Progress through all these steps before playing 6v6. When players are ready for full-court defensive drills, offer them an opportunity to play defense for an entire game or minigame. If they win, perhaps they get to be on defense again! This provides opportunities for repetition of defensive skills and emphasizes that defense is important. Give bonus points for a block or exceptional dig.

As a coach, you must make it clear that you treasure defense in order for players to crave it. Choose exciting defensive drills that give them the kind of thrill that attackers often experience.

Liberos can be the difference in a match. These specialized players who play back row only should be agile and quick. They should get more dig opportunities than others as well as more passing opportunities. Remember to include them while planning drills and to focus drills on them sometimes. If they are not an afterthought in practice, they will not be an afterthought in a match.

SPEED BALL

Purpose
To encourage players to be quick to receive the ball and to score on the opponent.

Setup
Three players spread out on each side of the court. The coach is off the court near the midline with a basket of balls and a feeder.

Run the Drill
1. The coach tosses the ball to a player on side B.
2. The player on side B catches the ball and immediately throws it to the opponents' side, attempting to score a point.
3. If a player on the receiving side is unable to catch the ball and throw it back, the team that threw the ball gets 1 point.
4. If a player on side A catches the ball, the player immediately throws it to the opponents' side, attempting to score a point.
5. This continues until one team scores 5 points (uncaught balls) by throwing to the opponents' open spots on the court.

Coaching Points
- To initiate play, start with a half-speed throw and increase velocity as players warm up.
- Emphasize the importance of reading the hitter or thrower.
- Teach your players to read the open areas of the opponents' court and develop court awareness.

Variation
Increase or decrease the number of points needed to win.

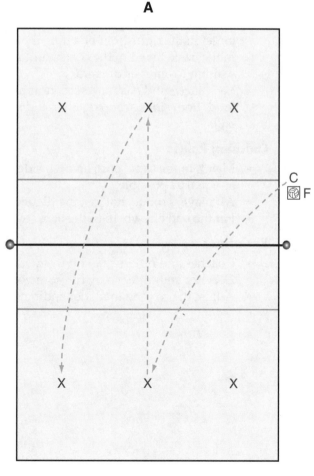

Purpose

To practice basic team defense within a given movement pattern.

Setup

Three players set up in the backcourt in defensive positions on side A, and three more set up in the backcourt on side B. One setter is on each side of the net. Extra setters can alternate or substitute on the coach's call. A target sets up in the right front. A coach or hitter is in the left-front position on each side. The hitter will hit at the three defensive players on the same side of the net. A cart of balls is on the side of the court near the coach. Extra players wait in a line on each side of the court.

Run the Drill

1. Each coach simultaneously hits, tips, or throws a ball to the defenders on the same side of the court.
2. Defenders dig to the setter, who sets a high ball back to the target in right front. The target catches the ball and places it in the cart then moves to the line.
3. Players rotate counterclockwise around the court after every attempt to dig, pass, and set, whether successful or not. After catching the ball as a target in the right-front position, the player leaves the court, puts the ball in the basket next to the coach, and goes to the end of the line of players waiting to enter as diggers.
4. Each successful pass and set counts as 1 point. Each target must count out loud. Both sides score together and strive to successfully set a total of 50 balls.

Coaching Points

- Maintain the same pace on each side to keep the line of off-court players as equal as possible.
- All players rotate, not just the diggers.
- Hit the ball anywhere in the backcourt.

Variations

- Coaches and hitters may hit from other positions along the net.
- Coaches and hitters may hit from boxes on the opposite side of the net.
- Adjust the scoring total, depending on the ability of the team.

A

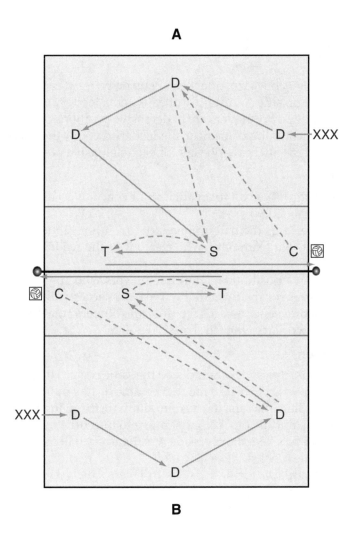

B

This drill is a tremendous opportunity to work on overlapping areas, verbal communication, and movement.

Purpose

To provide repeated opportunities for a team to dig balls on defense.

Setup

Two coaches or other consistent attackers set up on boxes at each outside-hitting position at the net on side A. A supply of balls and a feeder are on the sidelines near the net on side A. Six players are in defensive positions on side B. A score-keeper sets up outside the court near the feeder to count the successful digs. The coach preassigns alternate players for each defensive position.

Run the Drill

1. The feeder throws a ball to an attacker or coach, who hits or tips the ball over the net to side B.
2. The defender digs the ball up one foot (0.3 m) or higher off of the floor and sends it to a teammate, who clears it to the feeder on the opposite sideline.
3. Each defensive position has multiple players who stay on court only as long as it takes for the team to dig five balls successfully.
4. After the scorekeeper awards 5 points, the diggers rotate.
5. All players work together to score 100 points.

Coaching Points

- For beginners, the feeder should feed the same coach 5 to 10 balls in a row. Direct the middle blocker to move each time or stay outside for the series.
- For intermediate players, the feeders alternate throwing the ball to either attacker. The middle blocker must move to the correct side to block. The extra middle blockers stand on side A. After every ball or every three balls, a new middle blocker takes a turn.
- This is a fast-paced drill. Insist that players quickly return to the base position after each dig.
- Play to fewer than 100 as a goal for beginner players.

Variations

- When the skill level is appropriate, have the setter on side B catch or set every dug ball. A new setter steps in on every attacked ball.
- Use this as a transition drill and have players transition to attack on each ball. Because this lengthens the drill, you may need to decrease the goal.

A

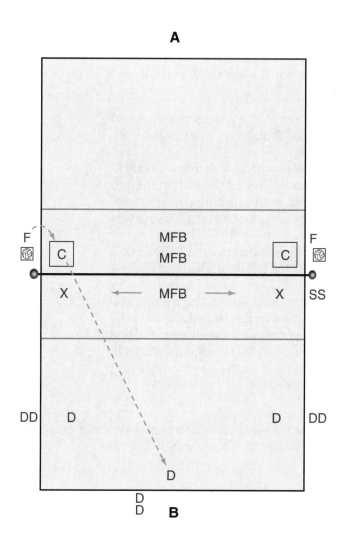

B

THREE-GUN SALUTE

This is a short-term, off-court drill for the early part of the season.

Purpose

To work on the preparedness and reaction time of each digger.

Setup

Groups of three set up at a solid wall in the gym. Each group has several balls.

Run the Drill

1. The first player in line sets up five to seven feet (about 1.5-2 m) from a flat, solid wall, facing it.
2. The second player or a coach throws a quick-paced ball underhand at the wall in front of the player hard enough to bounce off the wall.
3. The first player digs the ball up. Other players shag.
4. Repeat the action two more times. The second player throws the ball off the wall for the first player to dig.
5. Players rotate positions in the group. The first player goes to the end of the line, the second player becomes the digger, and the third player throws the ball against the wall.
6. Play continues with each player trying to dig three balls in a row.

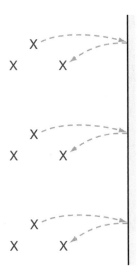

Coaching Point

Work on technique with individual players as they dig, emphasizing hands in front, low body position, and body weight forward.

Variations

- Vary the number of digs for each player.
- Add a setter.
- Move the defender a step to the left or right.

CHECK YOUR DISTANCE

Purpose

To help players establish a starting distance in relation to the net when blocking and to maintain that distance after moving.

Setup

One player begins at the net in the middle in a blocking ready position. Additional players line up behind the first. The coach sets up about five feet (1.5 m) from the net, facing the blocker.

Run the Drill

1. The first player performs a blocking sequence: block middle, block outside, block middle, block right side, block middle.
2. Each player takes a turn performing the blocking sequence.

Coaching Points

- Before the drill begins, perform a technical blocking checkup. Players should establish a blocking ready position, with elbows at the side and fingers extended and two inches (5 cm) from the net, and then move their hands high in front of the body.
- During the drill, check players' forearm position just before each block-jump.

Variation

Use any blocking sequence.

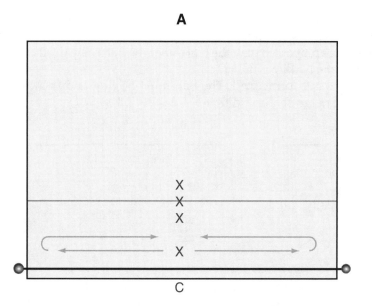

Besides providing repetitions, this is an instructional drill.

Purpose

To provide practice digging balls out of the net.

Setup

A coach and a basket of balls set up near the 10-foot (3 m) line. One player begins near the net in a low ready position. A line of players waits behind that player. A target player is in the middle of the court.

Run the Drill

1. The coach throws the ball into the top half of the net.
2. The player at the net digs the ball high into the middle of the court.
3. The target player catches the ball, gives it back to the coach, and gets in line to be the next player to dig out of the net.
4. Players take turns digging to the middle of the court until 24 balls are dug to the target.

Coaching Points

* Encourage players to see that when a ball goes into the top half of the net, it generally bounces out low and that a ball that goes into the lower half of the net generally bounces out high.
* Point out that pace and trajectory also determine where the ball will come out of the net.

Variations

* Challenge setters to set with the hands or to forearm-pass the ball out of the net to a target hitter.
* Challenge players to play the ball out of the net as the third contact, trying to send the ball over the net.
* Add a passer to the drill. The ball must be dug and then passed or hit over the net to score a point.

A

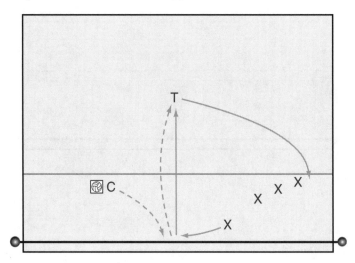

UNDER-THE-NET DIGGING

Purpose

To teach players to maintain a low position throughout the dig.

Setup

Two lines of players set up at the net on the sidelines of side A. Two coaches with a supply of balls are on side A. Target players set up on side B approximately five feet (1.5 m) in front of the diggers to catch the ball.

Run the Drill

1. The first player in each line moves in a low position toward the net.
2. Each coach hits a ball as the players approach the net.
3. The players dig the ball under the net to the target players.
4. The players who made the dig follow through onto side B and move around to the end of the line of players on the sidelines.

Coaching Points

- Because this is a technical instructional drill, do not run it for an extended time.
- After running this drill, during practice and in other drills, remind players to get low in the under-the-net position.

Variation

The players can start under the net with the coach near the net at the other side, forcing the player to move forward under the net all the way through the dig.

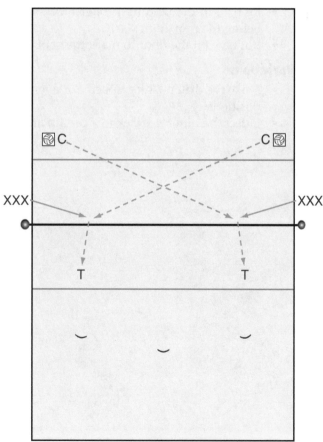

A

B

Players progress to making four transitions between offense and defense.

Purpose

To develop the transitions between front-row offense and defense.

Setup

Coach 1 is on a box at the net on side A with a basket of balls. Coach 2 is at the net on side B with a basket of balls. The first player starts at the net in blocking position. The rest of the players are off the court ready to enter when it is their turn.

Run the Drill

1. Coach 1 hits the ball at the first player, who attempts to block the ball.
2. The first player then transitions off the net and prepares to attack.
3. Coach 2 tosses a ball, and the first player attacks it.
4. The next player immediately gets in position to begin the drill by blocking a ball.
5. As players become skilled at making transitions, the coach extends the progression each player performs per turn: block to hit, then block to hit to block, then block to hit to block to hit.

Coaching Points

- Be firm in demanding proper blocking technique—players must block before the transition starts.
- Put tape on the floor to mark the spot the hitter must transition to.

Variations

- Make the drill position specific: Players should hit from their specialized positions.
- Direct the hitter's attack to a certain area of the court.

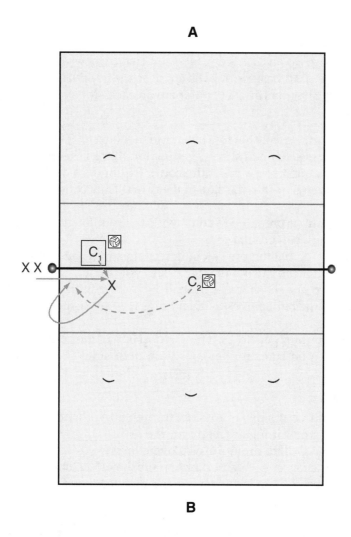

Purpose

To work on movement and conditioning, encouraging two players to cover the entire side of the court.

Setup

A pair of players set up on each side of the net. Two coaches at the net toss balls on their own side. Two baskets of balls are near the coaches, and two players feed the coaches. Shaggers and a counter are on each side.

Run the Drill

1. For the first round, coaches toss balls onto the court to open spaces, starting with easy tosses to open spaces, getting tougher as the drill progresses.
2. Two players must cover the entire court. Beginners start by catching the ball and tossing it off to the side of the court. They count until they catch 15 balls.
3. The next group is prepared to enter when the counter gets to 12 so no time is wasted between groups.
4. Players call the ball before catching it, not as they catch it. The counter does not count the catch if the player did not call it.
5. In round two, the coach tosses the ball, beginning with easy balls, and the player calls the ball, moves to it, and digs it to an assigned catcher at the net.
6. When the counter gets to 15, a new group enters the court.
7. The drill can be run simultaneously on both sides if there are enough players.

Coaching Points

- Make certain your skills in tossing, throwing overhand with two hands downward, and hitting are ready for the drill.
- Advance this drill to rapid fire as players improve.
- Give feedback after each group of two finishes 15 catches. If they are not showing success, stop immediately and give feedback.
- Have players practice digging without movement before adding movement.
- Focus on movement without bouncing up and down into different levels.

Variations

- Vary the number of players on the court. It is not always easier with more players. Calling the ball and maintaining aggressiveness with more players must be practiced.
- Add a setter: Dig and set 15 balls.
- Slowly advance to six players on the court.
- Add a team across the net and keep score. The coach enters the first ball to the digger.

A

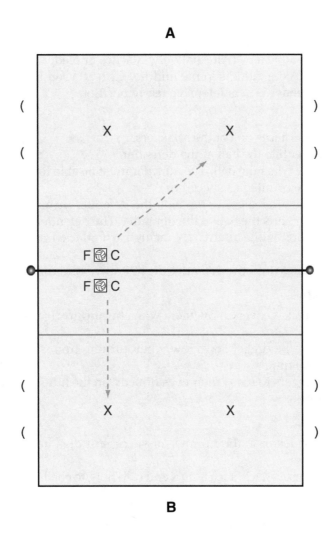

B

21-GUN SALUTE

Purpose
To improve defenders' reaction time.

Setup
Two attackers set up on the sidelines facing each other. A cart of balls is at each sideline, near the attackers. (Alternatively, coaches or feeder can provide balls to the attackers.) A defender is in the middle. Each attacker begins with a ball in hand. The defender is in a defensive ready position.

Run the Drill
1. The defender faces one of the attackers.
2. That attacker hits the ball at the defender.
3. The defender digs the ball. The attacker must be able to catch the ball for the dig to be counted as successful.
4. Immediately after digging the ball, the defender turns to face the other attacker, who hits the ball at the defender. The defender must stay in the ready position while alternately facing each attacker and attempting to dig the ball.
5. Play continues until the defender digs 21 successful digs.

Coaching Points
- Insist on quick recovery movement when turning to dig from the opposite side.
- Be sure that the digger stays low when turning from side to side to dig the opposite hitters.
- Remind diggers to focus their eyes directly on the hitter so their reaction time is quicker.

Variations
- Increase or decrease the number of successful digs necessary to finish the drill.
- Vary the type of attack, such as tips and roll shots, to challenge the defender.

A

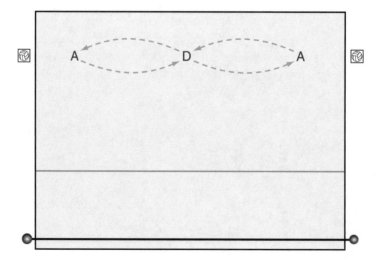

Purpose

To warm up or to practice secondary defense as a team, including movement, transition, and defensive skills.

Setup

Three backcourt players set up in defensive positions. A coach or hitter is in the right front and a defender is in the left front. (A more advanced team can place an additional coach or hitter in the left front on side A.) A setter is at the net in zone 6. Extra players line up near each position, ready to substitute. A feeder with a basket of balls sets up on the side of the court at the net.

Run the Drill

1. The coach or hitter sends an attack to the backcourt defenders.
2. Players dig the ball to the setter who sets the coach.
3. The coach again attacks the defenders.
4. Players repeat continuously, trying to keep the ball in play. The coach varies the attacks on the defenders.
5. The off-court substitutes count each hit out loud.
6. After four hits and four digs, substitutes switch on the run. Players who were on the court go to the end of the substitute line for their position.
7. The goal is to consistently keep the ball in play, transitioning to base after each attack.
8. Coaches can run this simultaneously on both sides of the net.

Coaching Point

To make the drill more fun and challenging, create a competition allowing players to stay on the court until they err twice, counting successful digs.

Variation

The drill can be run simultaneously on both sides of the court. Players on one side of the net can compete against the other, counting successful digs total or in a row.

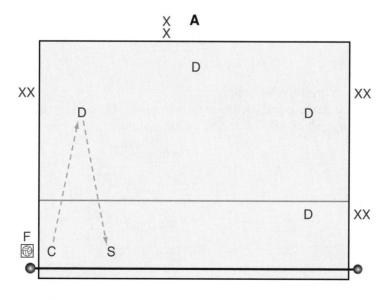

Purpose

To give the defense the opportunity to follow the offensive ball movement and to practice using a priority-based system of defense.

Setup

Six players set up on side A in defensive positions. Six players set up on side B in offensive positions. The coach is on the sideline with a supply of balls and a feeder.

Run the Drill

1. The coach tosses the ball over the net to side B.
2. Side B has the following options:
   - Pass the first ball back over.
   - Pass and then the setter dumps the ball.
   - Pass, set, and attack quickly.
   - Pass, set, and hit outside.
3. Side A responds using the following priority-based system for defense in this order:
   - Prepare for an errant pass coming immediately over the net.
   - Focus on the opposing setter for a second-ball attack or dump.
   - Prepare for a quick attack.
   - Prepare for the outside attack if the quick attack does not occur.
4. Side A digs the ball. The setter on side B catches the ball and rolls it off court to the shagger near the feeder.
5. The coach immediately initiates the next toss.
6. Play continues, with the offense executing different plays for the defense to react to, until the predetermined time limit or number of balls or attacks is reached.

Coaching Points

- Focus only on the defensive priority system, making certain that the defense responds according to the four steps of movement outlined in the drill.
- A second coach can call out to side B which offensive option to use for each ball.

Variations

- Side A can initiate play with a serve.
- Use game scoring and continue the rally until the ball is dead.
- Play short games, alternating sides for defense.

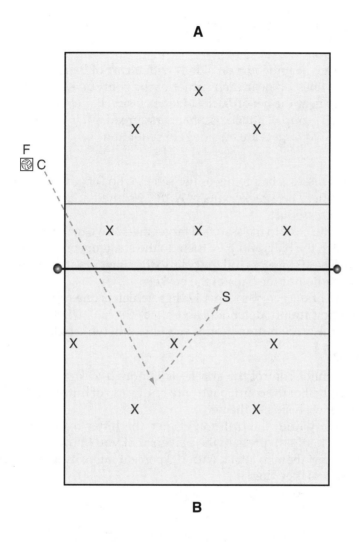

This is an early-season technical drill.

Purpose

To dig down-the-line attacks and crosscourt attacks repeatedly.

Setup

Two coaches set up at midcourt on side B with a cart of balls and a feeder. A group of diggers lines up near each corner of the court on side A. A group of attackers lines up near the net on each sideline on side B. The coach designates one setter for each group of attackers. Shaggers spread out in the middle of the court on side A. Two targets are on side A in setter zone 6.

Run the Drill

1. Each coach tosses a ball to his or her setter, who sets the first hitter from his or her line. The attacker hits only the assigned attack, such as down the line or crosscourt.
2. Defenders dig balls to the assigned target then move to the end of the line.
3. Targets catch the balls and give them to the shaggers on the same side of the court. These shaggers roll the balls to the shaggers at the opposite side of the net, who put the balls in the baskets.
4. Each group of diggers performs 12 digs, which is one round.
5. After the first round, defenders and attackers can switch positions and repeat, or the same hitting groups can hit a different angle.

Coaching Points

- If hitters cannot control the attack well enough to keep the ball on the designated half of the court, have only one group of hitters and defenders working on each side of the net.
- Competition within the drill might give the hitter reason to make the attack easy to dig. Express to the players that you know this is possible, but you expect them to attack with 100 percent intensity and you will not count it unless they do.
- Designate someone to count the digs.

Variation

Add a setter to side A. A successful score includes a dig and a set to a target.

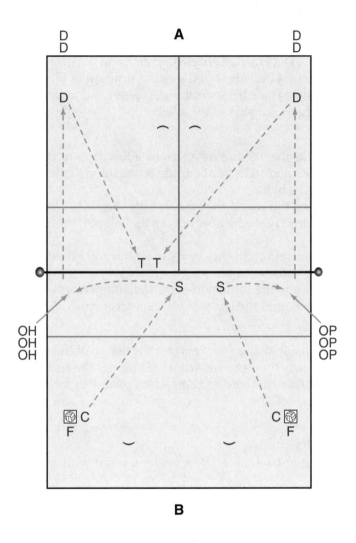

Purpose

To train the right front and right back to work together to defend first and then to communicate who sets the second ball.

Setup

One right-front blocker, one right-back defender, and two left-side attackers set up on side A. The first outside is at the net in position to block. A coach is on side B on a box in the right-front position. A feeder and a cart of balls are next to the coach. Shaggers spread out on side B.

Run the Drill

1. The coach hits the ball to side A's right side of the court.
2. The right back and right front on side A transition to their defensive positions to dig the ball.
3. After blocking the coach, the outside hitter on side A transitions to hit.
4. The right-side player who does not dig the ball, sets the ball to the left-side hitter.
5. The right front and right back cover the hitter and immediately transition back to their defensive base.
6. Players continue the same pattern, alternating attacks to the right front and right back until the left-side attacker terminates 20 balls.

Coaching Point

Communicate to the left-side attackers that the tempo of the set may be different depending on whether it comes from the setter or the secondary setter and that they need to take that into account when planning the timing and angle of their approach.

Variations

- Add a middle attacker.
- Allow the right-back defender to score a point with an attack from the back row.

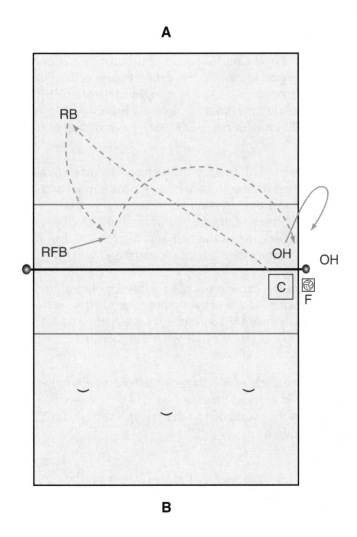

A

B

FIGURE 8

Purpose

To train defenders to run through balls and make sure their platforms face the target.

Setup

Coach 1 is at the net in the middle of the court on side A. Coach 2 is at the net in the middle of the court on side B. Six to eight players line up outside the court in the left-back corner on side A. Six to eight players line up outside the court in the right-back corner on side B. One target is on side A in position 6, and one target is on side B in position 6. Each coach has a basket of balls.

Run the Drill

1. Coach 1 tosses a ball toward the right-back corner of side A.
2. The first player in line at the left-back corner must accelerate to the right-back corner and pass the ball to the target.
3. After passing the ball, the passer immediately becomes the target.
4. Once the target catches the ball and puts the ball in the cart, the target must sprint to the other side of the court and enter the passing line in the right-back corner.
5. Coach 2 runs the same sequence on the opposite side of the court.
6. Players on both sides work together to pass 50 balls to the target.
7. Players loudly count the number of balls as they pass to the target so that the next player to pass knows what number that pass is.

Coaching Points

- Stress that the angle of the player's platform needs to face the target, which is the setter in zone 6 at the net.
- Insist on passing perfection from players, even while they are being physically challenged.

Variation

Increase or decrease the speed of the toss based on the number of players or the speed of the passer.

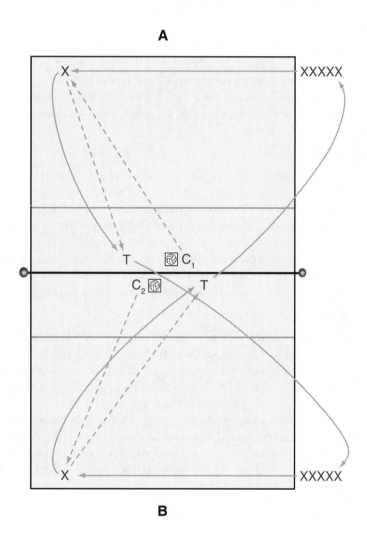

Purpose

To teach blockers to kill an overpass.

Setup

Right-front, middle-front, and left-front blockers set up on side A according to their position. Replacement blockers for each position set up behind the 10-foot (3 m) line. Three defenders set up on side B in the left back, middle back, and right back positions. A coach is on side B in the middle of the court with a cart of balls and a feeder. Players switch sides after the blockers reach five points or the diggers reach three.

Run the Drill

1. The coach tosses an overpass to the blockers, who try to terminate the ball.
2. The defenders must get two touches on the ball to negate the kill.
3. Once the blocker hits the overpass, that blocker switches places with the next blocker in line.
4. A successful overpass kill earns 1 point. Two touches on the ball by the defenders earn 1 point. An error by the blockers results in a loss of 1 point. Attackers try to terminate 10 balls before the defenders dig 6 balls.

Coaching Points

- Teach players that when a ball is between blockers, the player whose dominant hand is nearest the ball should attack the ball. For example, a ball tossed between the right front and middle front should be attacked by the middle, assuming that both players are right handed.
- Instruct the middles to be the most aggressive.
- Encourage your blockers to communicate on balls between two positions.
- Make sure that players drop-step, load, and attack the ball. This helps the blockers to stay behind the ball in order to attack it properly.
- Encourage your defenders if they are frustrated at first.

Variation

Have just one blocker at a time at the net.

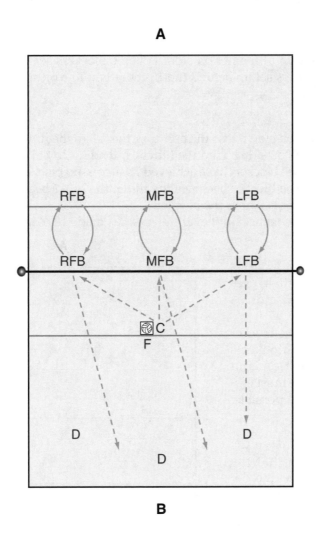

A

B

Purpose

To teach the blocker how to read the hitter, get into the correct position, and block the attack.

Setup

Three hitters set up at the net on side A. Three blockers set up at the net on side B. Three tossers set up behind the 10-foot (3 m) line on side B. Each has a cart of balls.

Run the Drill

1. The tossers on side B toss the ball over the net to the hitters on side A.
2. The blockers on side B read the hitters and adjust to block them.
3. Once the three blockers have achieved 10 successful blocks, players change positions. The blocker becomes the hitter, the hitter becomes the tosser, and the tosser becomes the blocker.
4. Repeat the sequence until every player has made 10 blocks.

Coaching Points

- Stress that the blockers must keep their eyes on the hitter and not the ball.
- Make sure the blocker starts in a blocker's ready position and moves in the most efficient manner possible.

Variation

Have the tosser move the hitter around so that the blocker must move in order to be properly positioned.

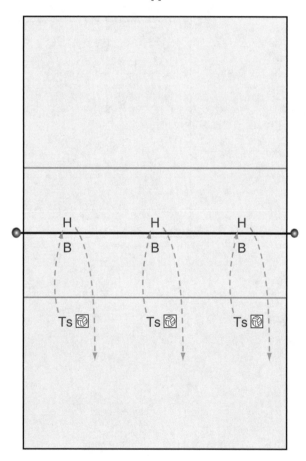

A

B

Purpose

To work on executing defensive technique and movement under pressure.

Setup

Three players set up on one side of the net: one player in that player's defensive base position, one at the net to act as the setter, and one in right front to act as the hitter. A coach is on the endline. A cart of balls is near the hitter on the sideline. The clock is set for 45 seconds.

Run the Drill

1. The hitter hits the ball at the defender, who passes to the setter at the net.
2. The setter sets the ball to the hitter, who again hits the ball at the defender.
3. This sequence continues until the time is up. If a ball is lost because of an error, a new one is taken from the basket.
4. Once the time has expired, players change positions: The hitter becomes the defender, taking the defensive position he or she normally plays, the setter becomes the hitter in right front, and the defender moves to take the setter position.
5. The drill runs for 45 seconds, then players rotate so that every player plays all three positions.
6. The hitter moves to the left-front position to simulate an attack coming from the opponents' right-front attacker. The sequence repeats.

Coaching Points

- Encourage players to work hard for the entire 45 seconds.
- Critique the defensive technique of the passer and defender during the drill using quick reminders such as "stay low" and "weight forward."

Variations

- Run the drill on both sides of the net.
- If you have four people in a group, make one a feeder, who can quickly send another ball to the hitter if an error occurs. Once time is up, the feeder rotates in and another player becomes the feeder.
- Increase or decrease the time period.

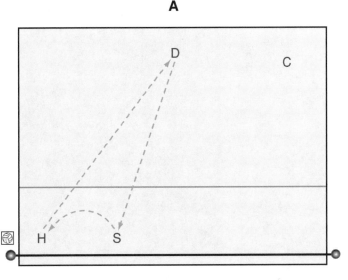

Purpose

To provide incentives for successful team defense by rewarding blocks.

Setup

Six players set up on both sides of the net. Players on side A are in their defensive positions. Players on side B are in their offensive positions. The coach is off court on side A with a cart of balls, a feeder, and a scorekeeper.

Run the Drill

1. The coach initiates a down ball or free ball to side B (the offense).
2. Players play out the rally.
3. The scorekeeper tracks blocks and stuff blocks as well as the winner of each rally.
4. One point is given to the winner of the rally. Side B wins points only by winning the rally. Side A can score by winning the rally but also earn additional points for blocks and stuff blocks. Side A receives 1 point for each blocked ball and 3 points for each stuff block (a ball that hits the ground immediately).
5. Side A must score 9 points before side B scores 6.

Coaching Points

- Encourage sound blocking technique.
- The scorekeeper must pay attention during each rally to give points for blocks.

Variations

- Side A may only score by stuff block. They must earn 3 points (one stuff block) before side B gets 3 points (three rallies)
- To increase the challenge, award bonus block points for both teams. Alternate which side gets the first ball. The first team to 9 points is the winner.

A

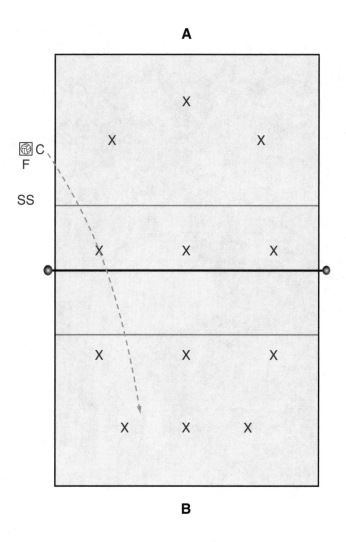

B

chapter 7

Transition Drills

Transitions in volleyball include the time spent moving from one skill to another and moving from defense to offense and back. A successful volleyball team practices transitions regularly, gaining precision and speed. Every player must know where to go and how to get there.

The team movement on the court should be marked by a focused but relaxed group flow. Transitional flow is a fluid shifting in which players seem to move as one and each player knows where and how to move in relation to the rest of the team. On a team with good flow, everyone moves at the same time with an efficiency, precision, and smoothness that make it look effortless.

> **Championship teams are champions of transition.**

Each player must move in the most efficient line possible and with little or no wasted energy. Coaches should spend time teaching individual movement patterns before running team transition drills. If every player knows where to go to cover after an attack and where to move in defensive play, the team's transitions will flow smoothly. A single player moving to an incorrect position or moving too slowly to that position interrupts the flow.

Players should move from a medium level, neither as high as for the serve nor as low as for the dig. In this position the knees are slightly bent so that players move with the help of the biggest muscles. Players should be light on their feet rather than loud and heavy. Encourage hitters to land on both feet and then transition to a blocking or low defensive position.

If players move in a high position, the transition is less efficient and more awkward because they will have to lower themselves to a defensive position when arriving at their next task.

Transition work should be done without the volleyball first and then with it. Walking through transition is a necessary part of learning. Repeat this until players can do it efficiently and proficiently and at game speed. Then add a ball.

Practice repetitions of each transition that occurs within the game of volleyball. The drills in this chapter focus on the time and movement between skills in the game. Some are individual in nature, such as working on a hitter transitioning to block after the attack and then transitioning back to the attack. Some drills focus on team transition, such as a team on offense with good hitter coverage and then transitioning to team defense with everyone moving to their base position and back to offense. The following drills teach players to make smooth, efficient, quick transitions. You will also find that transition work improves the running of multiplayer and team drills.

Coach, you will not regret making transition work a regular part of each practice. Teams with great championship history excel in transition work. These teams have flow and often win even when they are not as skilled as their opponent. Transition can win matches.

PULL DRILL

This is an outstanding drill for emphasizing proper footwork in a controlled situation. It is also a fantastic conditioning drill.

Purpose

To perfect the footwork for hitters' transition off the net and approach to attack.

Setup

Six hitters set up in the right front, middle front, and left front on both sides at the net in base position as if they were preparing to block. Coaches set up at the sideline near or behind the 10-foot (3 m) line.

Run the Drill

1. The player in the left front on side B calls "pull," and all six hitters transition off the net to their starting approach position and quickly approach for the attack.
2. Each player moves in a counterclockwise direction to the next base blocking position, ready to transition.
3. The new player in the left front position on side B initiates the next transition by calling "pull."
4. Players repeat the same pattern 12 times.

Coaching Points

- Monitor players' footwork and watch carefully to make sure they transition far enough off the net.
- Put tape or some type of marker on the floor for base blocking positions and approach starting positions.

Variation

Increase or decrease the number of transitions based on players' fitness levels.

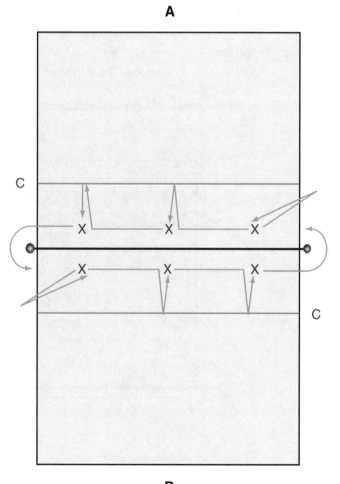

Purpose

To push the defender to the limit by challenging the defender to dig many balls in rapid succession.

Setup

Ten to twelve players, each with a ball, form a circle around one defender. The coach puts three minutes on the clock.

Run the Drill

1. Proceeding in a clockwise direction one at a time, each player around the circle hits a ball at the defender in the middle.
2. The defender digs the ball back to the hitter.
3. Each attacker must retrieve the ball that he or she hit at the defender, no matter where it is dug.
4. Play continues until the defender has dug 30 balls back to the attacker or the clock runs out.

Coaching Points

- Emphasize that shoulders and feet must be squared to the hitter.
- Be sure that the hitters keep a fast and steady pace that challenges the defender.

Variations

- Increase or decrease the number of successful digs needed or the duration of the drill.
- Have attackers hit roll shots and tips.

A

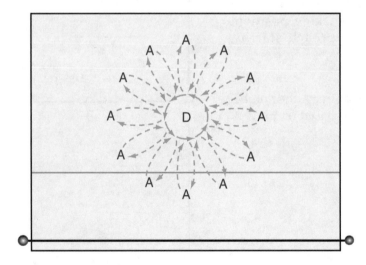

You can run just about any drill without a ball. In this example, we use an offense vs. defense.

Purpose

To check skills, movement, positioning, covering, and transition.

Setup

Three front-row attackers set up on the 10-foot (3 m) line on side A. A setter is at the net and a passer is in the back row. Six players get into defensive positions on side B. A tosser sets up off the court on side B.

Run the Drill

1. The tosser initiates the imaginary ball over the net to the passer on side A.
2. Side A passes, sets, and hits the imaginary ball.
   - Hitters call to the setter for the set.
   - Defenders call out "line" or "cross" based on the position of the hitter.
3. The team on side B transitions to offense and plays the imaginary ball out, calling out the action for all to follow.

Coaching Points

- Run the drill at match pace. Player movement, or the lack thereof, is easier to observe when no ball is used.
- Halt the drill as needed to perform checkups and provide feedback.
- Players must call the ball, call the attack, and communicate on defense and use proper form. Provide feedback.
- Use this drill to check movement, transition, and other skills during any part of the season. However, for greatest effect, do not perform a no-ball drill more than twice a season.

Variations

- Run any drill without a ball.
- Run an entire practice session without balls.

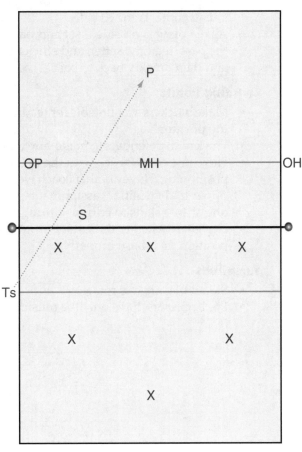

This is an excellent drill for practicing transitions on one side of the net while practicing setting and passing repetitions on the other. It is also good for encouraging blocker communication and promoting player conditioning.

Purpose

To read, respond, and transition from defense to offense.

Setup

Six players set up in base defense on side A. A setter gets into position 6 on side B. One player sets up in position 1 and another in position 9 on side B. A third player sets up in the middle back on side B.

Run the Drill

1. The coach tosses the ball to the setter on side B.
2. The setter on side B sets either a front set to the player in position 1 or a back set to the player in offensive position 9.
3. The player who receives the initial set then sets the ball to the player in the middle back.
4. The player in the middle back passes the ball to the setter in position 6 on side B.
5. The players on side B stay in their positions and continue this sequence of ball contacts for 10 balls.
6. As the players on side B set and pass the ball, the players on side A read the pass, read the setter, and efficiently move to their defensive positions and then quickly back to base.

Coaching Points

- Make blockers accountable for reading the setter before releasing to blocking position.
- Work with defenders to make sure they are in the right position for the set.
- Have one coach work with the defenders on reading, transitioning, and positioning. Have another coach work with blockers to critique footwork, upper-body position, assignments, and lining up on the attacker. Choose one or two skills to critique during the 10 balls.
- Designate whether the setter is front row or back row so that your blockers position their base properly.

Variations

- Side B players can rotate.
- For beginners, have only the outsides set and hit down balls over the net.

A

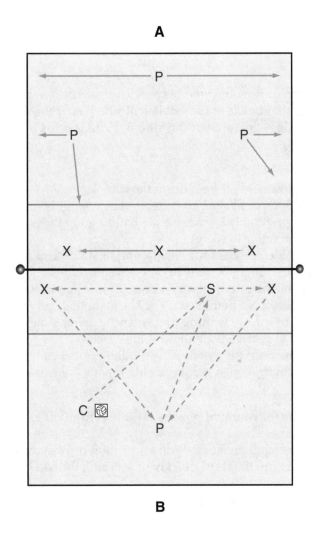

B

This drill introduces small-group transition. Coaches can better focus on individual transition strengths and weaknesses.

Purpose

To allow players to practice transitioning while attempting to score more points than their opponents.

Setup

The coach creates groups of three players. (If needed, one team or more can have four players.) A ball is at the sideline of side B near the coach. A group of three starts on side A and another on side B. Extra groups line up behind the endline on side A.

Run the Drill

1. The coach enters a ball over the net to side A.
2. Rally continues until the ball is dead. (For young, beginning teams, it is sometimes preferable to require the ball to go between the endline and attack line in order to score).
3. Players on side A focus on transitioning to attack and set positions after the initial pass. Team B starts in defensive positions.
4. If side B wins the rally, it scores a point. If side A wins the rally, it simply moves to side B. No point is scored. The team that lost the rally moves to the endline of side A, waiting to reenter the game. A new team advances to the court to receive the ball from the coach.
5. Triples teams keep their own scores, calling out each time they score.
6. The first team to score 6 points on side B wins the game.

Coaching Points

- Focus on the transition of players on side A from offense to defense and back to offense.
- This is a lead-up to 6v6 transition (Transition or Bust drill).
- Move teams onto the court quickly by entering the ball quickly. They will catch on.
- Because the teams keep their own scores, do a score check once in a while.

Variations

- Run this as a 3v6 drill.
- Initiate the drill from a serve from team B if players can pass efficiently. Because the emphasis is on transition, do this only if your players can put the ball in play most of the time.

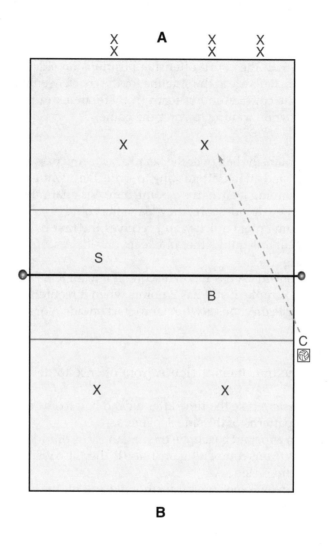

Purpose

To give the team the opportunity to transition from offense to defense and back to offense.

Setup

Players set up 6v6 on the court: offensive positions on side A and defensive positions on side B. Balls are at the sideline for the coach to enter. A scorekeeper is at the side of the court. Another team (if there are extra players) can shag around the court while waiting to enter the game.

Run the Drill

1. The coach enters the ball over the net to a back-row passer on side A. Players pass, set, and attack, attempting to score. Play continues until the rally ends. The winning team earns a point. Side A is guaranteed two attempts to score. If they do not score, they leave the court.
2. The new team enters quickly and receives the first ball from the coach. Players repeat this until either one team on side A scores 6 points or side B scores 8.
3. Each team on side A has its own score. If a team leaves the court with 2 points, for example, it still has 2 points when it reenters the court.
4. The winning team chooses whether to start on side A or side B for the next game.

Coaching Points

- Focus on the transition of side A from offense to defense and back to offense.
- When necessary, take the time after a dead ball to correct positioning or movement patterns of the side A players.
- If there is an assistant coach, he or she can focus on side B transition.
- While side A teams compete against side B, they also want to score 6 before the other team on side A.
- Encourage an extremely fast transition on and off the court for teams on side A by entering the ball quickly.

Variations

- If you do not have enough players for two complete teams on side A, use three players.
- If you have only 12 players, have side A players switch front and back rows every 2 points, but score it as one team.
- Play the game to different numbers of points. This encourages immediacy of scoring. Varying the end score keeps the competitive level high.

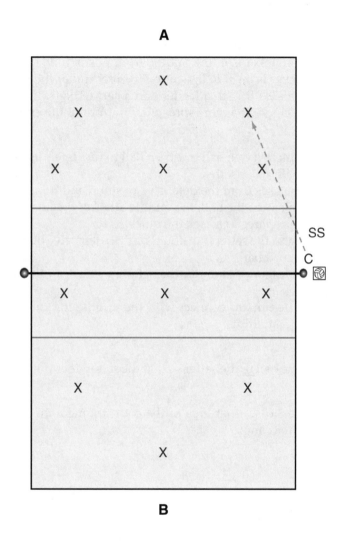

Purpose
To train the setter to transition from defense to offense.

Setup
A setter sets up in the right back on side A. A defender is in the middle back on side A. A middle attacker is in the middle front position on side A. A replacement middle attacker is on side B, waiting to enter under the net. A coach sets up at midcourt on side B with a feeder and a cart of balls. If timing the drill, the coach sets the clock. Shaggers spread out in front of the endline of side B.

Run the Drill
1. The coach enters a free ball or down ball to the defender on side A, who passes the ball to the setter.
2. The setter releases from the defensive position and transitions to the net.
3. As the coach enters the ball, the middle attacker on side A transitions off the net and prepares to attack the quick set.
4. After the attack, the setter transitions back to defensive base, and the coach initiates the next ball.
5. The next middle moves under the net onto side A and becomes the next middle attacker.
6. The setter attempts to connect with the middle for 10 balls within two minutes or 15 attempts.

Coaching Point
Occasionally hit the ball to the setter so that the setter does not release too early.

Variation
Move the defender to another area of the court to make the setter and hitter adjust to the different angle.

A

B

Purpose

To work on defensive transition as a team.

Setup

Six defenders set up on side B. A setter is in zone 6 at the net on side A, and two target players are on each side of the setter in zones 1 and 9. A passer is in the middle-back position. A coach is on the sideline with a cart of balls.

Run the Drill

1. The coach tosses a ball to the passer on side A.
2. The passer on side A passes to the setter on side A, who either back-sets or front-sets the ball.
3. The defense on side B transitions from base to defense, according to the location of the set. For example, if the set goes to the target in the left front position, then the defense transitions to defend that set.
4. The target sets the ball back to the passer, who passes the ball to the setter.
5. Play continues until the designated number of transitions has been completed.

Coaching Points

- Make sure the defense waits until the set is made to move to defensive positions. Do not let them cheat and leave early.
- In this drill, the defenders should work very hard. Give them consistent feedback on where they should be.
- Change out the middle blocker every three to five balls.

Variation

Move the setter to zone 9 at the net and use a middle hitter.

A

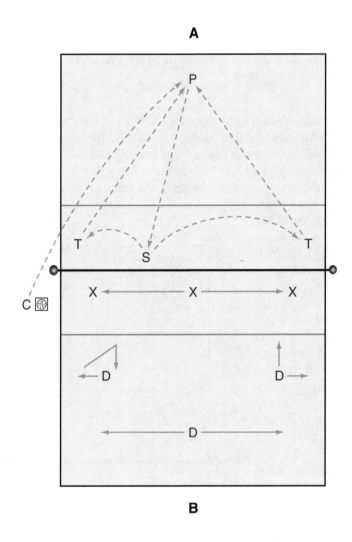

B

Purpose

To score with defensive transition, beginning with the serve

Setup

The players set up 6v6 on the court. Another group of six can be waiting off court, shagging balls. Balls are at the endline of side A, and a scorekeeper is at the sideline.

Run the Drill

1. Team A initiates the ball with a serve.
2. The goal of team A is to either block or transition from defense to offense, scoring immediately on the transitional ball. This scores 1 point.
3. Play continues until the ball is dead; however, team A can only score on the first transition opportunity. Team B can score on any play it wins.
4. Back-row players alternate serving. As soon as the serve is made, all players on side A transition to their defensive positions (if necessary).
5. Players do not rotate during the game.
6. The serving team must score 6 points by serving and scoring on the first ball-handling opportunity, discouraging a continued rally. When one team wins the game, it stays on the court and the waiting team enters to play them. The team that won the first game is the serving team. The team goes to the serving end and becomes team A for the next game.
7. The teams repeat the drill several times. Each time the team plays a new game, the front and back rows switch places.

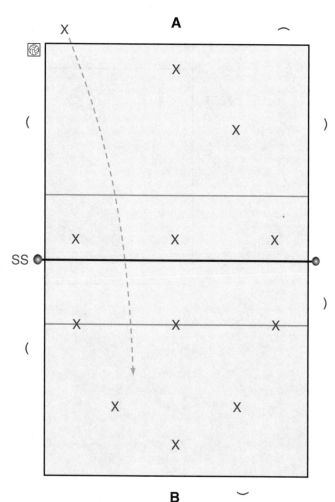

Coaching Points

- Focus on the transition of players on team A to defensive positions and then to offensive positions. If you have one, an assistant can focus on team B's transition. It is more effective, even with one coach, to focus on the transition of only one side of the court. This is the purpose of the drill.
- While players on side A can only score on the first transition, it is necessary for them to continue at full effort if they do not score in order to keep side B from scoring on continued rallies.
- This is a highly competitive drill.
- Remember that low-scoring systems like this give many opportunities for victories, thus encouraging competitive spirit.

Variations

- When playing several games, a good variation is to play two games to only 2 points, then two games to 4 points, and then two games to 6 points. This can continue or start over. Players experience the immediacy of transitioning effectively on the first point.
- If fewer than 12 players are at a practice, put 6 players on side A and 3 or more on side B. Play with the same procedures. If you have more than 18 players, maintain just three teams, but use subs, who alternate every two served balls with a preassigned player on the court.
- If a big match is looming late season, give more opportunity on side A to those who will see more court time in the match. This is fine because alternates can exchange places only on side B.
- Rotate players throughout the drill or each time they enter a new game.

This structured drill works on every aspect of outside hitting. It's a great conditioning drill for the outsides because they must transition hard. Defenders must set the ball consistently.

Purpose

To focus on the transition by the outside hitters from their blocking position, to defense, to offense, and to hitting a controlled attack.

Setup

A front-row setter, an outside hitter, and a left-back defender set up on side A. A front-row setter, an outside hitter, and a left-back defender set up on side B. A coach is on the sideline on side B with a cart of balls.

Run the Drill

1. The coach enters a free ball to the left back on side A.
2. Players on side A pass, set, and attack the ball crosscourt to the team on side B.
3. Side B digs, sets, and attacks the ball across the net to side A.
4. This cooperative drill continues until 12 attacks across the net have been completed.
5. The setters block the line to make the hitter hit crosscourt.

Coaching Points

- This is not an all-out hitting drill, but players should attack the ball with pace. Hitters should maintain the speed of their approach and adjust the speed of the arm swing.
- Emphasize communication between the outside and left-back defender.
- Alternate the setters so that the outsides have to work with both or all of them.

Variations

- Add or decrease the number of successful attacks necessary to complete the drill.
- If players are not completing the drill, set a time limit after which you replace the outsides.
- Integrate tips and roll shots to increase the challenge.

A

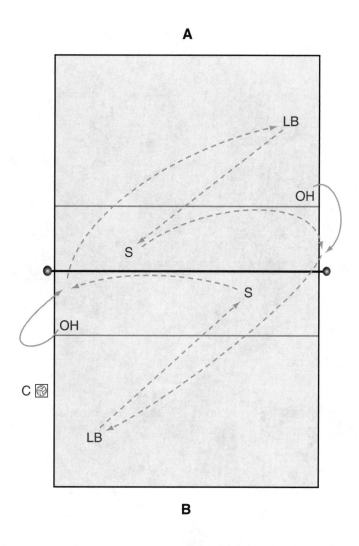

B

Competitive Multiplayer Drills

Connecting with teammates in a competitive environment is what *team* play is all about. It's why athletes play a team sport. To an athlete, adding the multiplayer dimension to a drill invites camaraderie and increases the incentive to perform well in the drill. The athletes want to win not only for themselves but also for their teammates.

Many athletes are self-driven to compete. Some are more inspired by playing with teammates. Whether players are strongly self-motivated or motivated mainly by their teammates, they choose volleyball because they are looking to participate in *group* play. It is imperative to run individual skill drills and do so with high repetition, but it is equally important to provide opportunity for players to perform those skills in combination drills with others. Because volleyball is a team sport, it is valuable to add the multiplayer drills as soon as possible.

Adding a scoring system to drills is essential. Trying to score more points than the opponent is the goal in every volleyball game. It only makes sense that players would want to do this in practice. Coaches must provide opportunities to win.

Multiplayer drills offer the opportunity to compete while keeping the focus on skill development. The emphasis may be on the pass in serve receive, yet players are also invited and encouraged to compete for victory. Players compete as a group and for the group. These drills encourage cohesiveness. They invite some players to step up as leaders and others to follow. They allow coaches to discover who responds well to pressure situations, who performs specific skills better in game situations, and who needs more individual work.

When the drill is general and the composition of the groups does not matter, use fun methods to form the groups. To make teams, play a game such as Klumpers, in which the coach yells a number and players scramble to huddle into groups of that number of players. Or group players by hair color, height, age, birthdates—variety is good. When the composition of each group matters, such as when a particular offensive lineup is needed or when players must be grouped according to position or ability, determine groups in advance. This saves managerial and transition time in practice.

> Competitive multiplayer drills allow players to focus on and improve their individual skills while learning to be accountable to the group and to work together in order to be successful. The sooner players experience group play, the sooner they learn to cooperate, assist, and support each other.

Perform multiplayer drills during every phase of the season. You can use endless scoring methods, adaptations, and variations to keep things interesting. These drills are the core of the program. They offer players lots of repetitions of skills, but because the repetition is done with teammates and in a competitive setting, the reps are more meaningful and more fun. Players love the chance to bond and to win.

It is not necessary to reward winners. Winning *is* the reward! Celebrating the win briefly is a gift to the players, however. Show them that you recognize the victory. It is also effective to sometimes recognize the winner with more of the skill. Winners might get to remain on the court with no substitutions the next round while the opponent is subbed, for example, or a group that wins the Offensive vs. Defense drill can choose whether to start on offense or defense.

It is not necessary to punish the losers. Not being recognized as winners is sufficient.

Remember that the most gamelike incentive is the win itself. When a group is simply happy to win and needs no further incentive, it is clear that they understand much of what teamwork is about—achieving victory *together*.

Purpose

To practice setting various attacks against a full-team defense.

Setup

Six players set up on side A in a full-team defense. Three lines of two attackers set up in each position on side B. A setter is at the net on side B. A coach with a cart of balls is behind the 10-foot (3 m) line on side B.

Run the Drill

1. The coach tosses to the setter on side B.
2. The setter sets to the left, middle, or opposite attacker.
3. The attacker attempts to score on the defense by making a kill. The defense attempts to score on the attackers by digging and setting to a hitter, who catches the ball.
4. Whenever a team scores, players yell out the first or next letter in the word "champions." Play continues until one team completes the word.
5. When a setter sets a hitter, all three hitters are replaced. Hitters keep alternating.

Coaching Points

- Encourage all players to keep track of scoring letters.
- Beginners can hit all high sets.

Variations

- Add slide hits and X plays for more advanced players.
- Side B can run free-ball plays or serve-receive plays against the defense instead of using attack lines.
- Add covering of the attacker if players are ready for that.
- You can assign specific attacks that players need to work on or allow hitters to call their attacks.

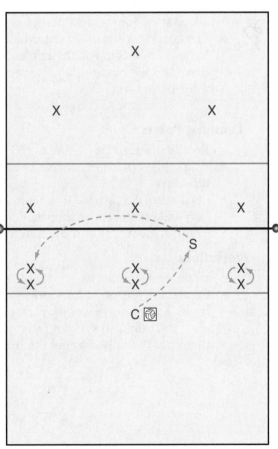

TRIPLES TROPHY

Purpose

To provide a competitive opportunity for players to make multiple contacts in match play with playing time as the incentive.

Setup

The coach divides the team into groups of three, based on position: for example, one outside hitter, one middle hitter, and one setter or opposite. Four groups of three begin on the court, two groups on each side of the net. Extra groups wait at the sideline. A coach or tosser is at the side of the court with a cart of balls. The coach designates one of the hitters per team to be the scorekeeper.

Run the Drill

1. The two groups on each side of the net play as a team. If there is more than one setter per team, the back-row setter sets.
2. The coach enters the ball, and the teams compete.
3. When the rally ends, the group of three who erred moves to the end of the off-court line.
4. A new group of three moves onto the vacated front or back of the side that lost the last rally.
5. The two groups on the side of the net that won the rally each get 1 point and stay on for the next point.
6. The coach continues to enter balls, and play continues until one team scores 12 points to win the Triples Trophy. That team gets to choose where they start the next round. The second-place team chooses next, then the third-place team.
7. Teams continue to compete for three or four rounds.

Coaching Points

- Enter balls quickly.
- Allow players to get excited, but encourage quick transitions on and off the court.
- Do a score check once in a while. It reminds players to keep score and keeps the scorekeepers honest.
- This is a great first introduction to competitive play.

Variations

- Have the teams serve.
- Create a bonus point for scoring on a particular type of attack.
- If you have 12 or fewer players, everyone plays. The team of three who wins the rally stays in the same positions and scores a point. The team that loses the rally changes the front row with the back row.

A

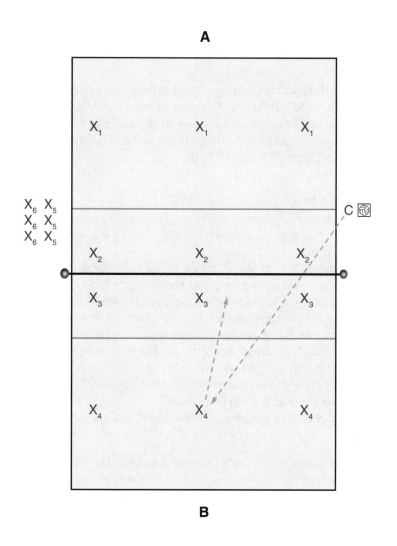

B

This is an effective introductory-level or higher competitive drill.

Purpose

To allow players to get in many repetitions by competing in position and working cooperatively with other players.

Setup

The coach divides the team into groups of three based on position: for example, an outside hitter, a middle hitter, and a setter or opposite hitter. Four groups of three players begin on the court, two groups on each side of the net. The outside hitters serve as the scorekeepers. Extra groups wait on the endline on side B. A coach is on the sideline with a cart of balls.

Run the Drill

1. The coach enters the ball to either side.
2. The two groups on each side of the net play as a team.
3. Teams rally until the ball is dead. Both groups of players on the winning side score a point.
4. The coach enters a second ball to the other side. Again teams rally until the ball is dead, and both groups on the winning side score a point.
5. After two rallies in the same position (a ball initiated to each side), all groups "wave" through the court to a new position by advancing toward the endline on side A. A new group enters in the back row on side B, the back row on side B becomes the front row, the front row from side B moves to the front row on side A, and the front row from side A takes the back row. The group from the back row of side A leaves the court and goes to the end of the line at the side B endline.
6. Play continues until a group of three wins 15 points.

Coaching Points

- Insist on fast-paced transitions between the drill. If players do not switch quickly, enter the ball anyway to force players to get into position quickly.
- Evaluate players in the same position as they work their way through the court. Watch to see how well players adjust to working with a new group.

Variation

Some competitive groups might not help a group with 14 points to win the final point. Rather than insist they help, give the group of three with 14 points the option of playing alone on the court for the final point.

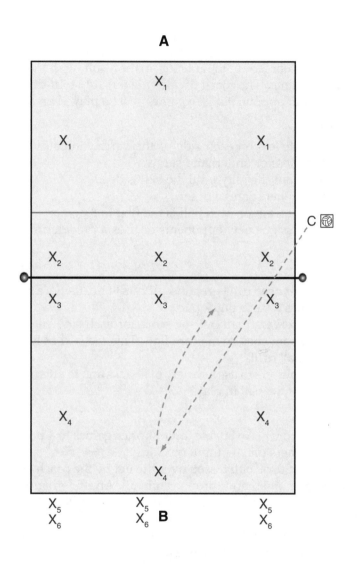

Purpose

To give players the opportunity to touch a lot of balls in a competitive game.

Setup

The court is divided in half lengthwise from 10-foot (3 m) line to 10-foot line, using removable floor tape or the antenna. In the resulting short court, the 10-foot lines are the end lines. The coach divides players into four doubles teams and assigns courts and opponents. Two games will be played on each court.

Run the Drill

1. One of the teams on each side of the barrier initiates the ball with an underhand toss or underhand serve.
2. Teams play out the rally until the ball is dead.
3. The rally winner scores a point.
4. The winning team on each half is the first to 8 points.
5. The coach assigns new opponents or uses a predetermined tournament format.

Coaching Points

- This is a fast-paced drill—remind players to hustle. Set a two-minute limit on the games to set a quick pace.
- Have the "servers" call out the score for each side before initiating the ball, calling out their own score first. This method of keeping score can be used for all drills.
- Encourage players to use a variety of attacks and to attempt to score rather than just put the ball in play.

Variations

- If only one court is available, play shorter games to 4 points.
- Have beginners play without blocking.
- Start with a 50/50 ball tossed over the net by the coach.
- Start with an overhand throw or hit ball. An underhand serve or toss is preferable even at advanced levels because the drill is about ball handling.
- If you have a large number of players, put three to five players in a group and have them quickly rotate after every dead ball.
- With a small number of players, have players compete 1v1, with each player receiving three contacts.

A

B

This is a good preseason drill.

Purpose

To improve serving and passing accuracy through numerous repetitions.

Setup

Servers line up on the endline on side B with a supply of balls. Two players are in line at the sideline of side A. Three passers prepare to serve-receive on side A, and a target player sets up in zone 7. The coach starts the timer.

Run the Drill

1. The first server serves to side A.
2. The receiving player passes the ball to the target player, who catches it.
3. After the ball is passed and the target catches it (no bounces allowed), the target rotates to the serving line on side B. The passer from the farthest right-back position becomes the target. The other passers move one position to the right, and a new passer enters from the sideline. The server goes to the end of the line at the sideline on side A. The rotation needs to be fast.
4. Players immediately repeat the sequence.
5. Play continues until 100 balls have been caught. Note the time.
6. Establish that time as the goal to beat.

Coaching Points

- Keep the transitions quick.
- Encourage stronger players to serve with pace to reduce the time the ball is in the air and to keep the action moving quickly.

Variation

Add a setter in the target position who stays in place and sets to a target in a given hitting position. Instead of rotating to the target position, the passer rotates to the hitting position before going to serve. The setter remains constant.

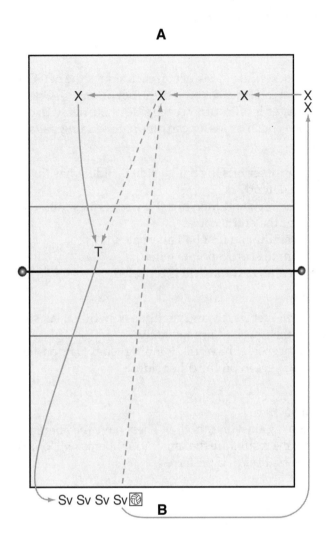

Purpose

To work on transition at the net from offense to defense and back; to give the libero the opportunity to dominate defensive play and coverage; to work on setter transition.

Setup

Three hitters or blockers are at the net on each side of the net. One setter is in the backcourt on side A; another setter is at the net on side B. One libero is on each side. A coach or tosser is off court on each side of the net with balls and a feeder. (Alternatively, one coach or tosser can alternate sending balls to each side.)

Run the Drill

1. The coach or tosser hits the ball to side B. Side A has three blockers at the net ready to defend.
2. Side B passes, sets, and then hits. Play continues until the ball is dead.
3. Liberos cover the entire court.
4. The side receiving the first ball alternates.
5. The first team to score 8 points wins.
6. Substitutes enter, and the drill is repeated.

Coaching Points

- Keep the drill fast paced and highly competitive. As soon as the ball is dead, enter the next ball immediately.
- For added incentive, have the winning team stay on the court and put substitute players in on the other side.

Variations

- Add a full back row.
- Pit the liberos against one another. Then, have the liberos switch sides and see whether the results are the same. Your liberos will love the competition!
- Run set free-ball plays if preferred.

A

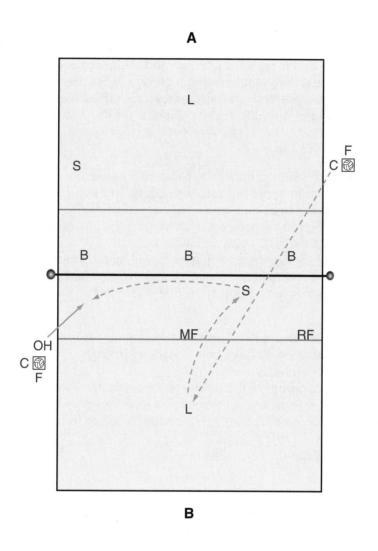

B

Purpose

To give players practice in playing six-person defense and transitioning to offense.

Setup

One passer (who covers both the left back and middle back on defense), three attackers, and one setter get into position on side A. Six players set up on side B in their defensive positions. A coach or tosser is off the court on side B with a supply of balls and a feeder. A scorekeeper is off the court, close to but not right at the net.

Run the Drill

1. The coach or tosser initiates the ball to the passer on side A. The tosser can toss, pop, or serve the ball, depending on the passer's skill level or the type of skill to be worked on.
2. Players on both sides pass, set, and hit, with the hitters calling out the set they want as the teams play out the rally.
3. The team of six has the advantage of a full team. Strong transition from defense to offense will be rewarded, making it easier to score.
4. The rally winner earns 1 point. The first side to score 6 points is the winner.

Coaching Points

- Assign substitutes for the defensive players on side B before the drill. Substitute after every three balls the tosser initiates or wait and sub in a full team of defenders.
- You can have groups of three players wave onto the court for new games: The front row from side A moves to the front row of side B, the front row of side B moves to the back row, and the back row from side B moves to the front row of side A.
- Plan your teams for several games.

Variations

- Add a full team to side A.
- Work only on specific attacks from side A.
- Keep the same attackers together and put them with different setters to compare the effectiveness of the setters within the drill.

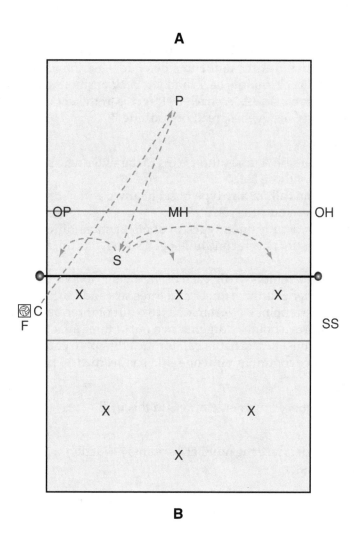

Purpose

To give hitters the opportunity to improve their shot selection.

Setup

Two hitters of the same or different positions begin on side A. A setter sets up on side A in position 6 at the net. Three defenders get into defensive base on side B in the right back, middle back, and left back positions. A coach or tosser is in the backcourt on side A. A coach or target is at the net on side B to catch the defenders' digs. Shaggers spread out on side B.

Run the Drill

1. The coach on side A tosses three balls to the setter who sets the first hitter on all three of those balls.
2. The hitter can call for any type of set at any position on the court, or the coach can designate the set.
3. The hitter must hit three types of shots at three different speeds. For example, a hitter may hit one full-speed swing, one tip, and one off-speed roll shot.
4. The defense attempts to dig each of the swings to the coach on side B.
5. The next hitter gets three tosses and three sets and executes three swings.
6. Hitters score a point by terminating two out of three balls in each series. Defense scores a point by digging two out of three attacks from the hitter. A dug ball must be a settable ball for the attempt to count.
7. The sequence continues until one side has accrued 10 points.

Coaching Point

Use outside, middle, or right-side hitters in this drill.

Variations

- Increase or decrease the number of points needed to win.
- Add live passers.

A

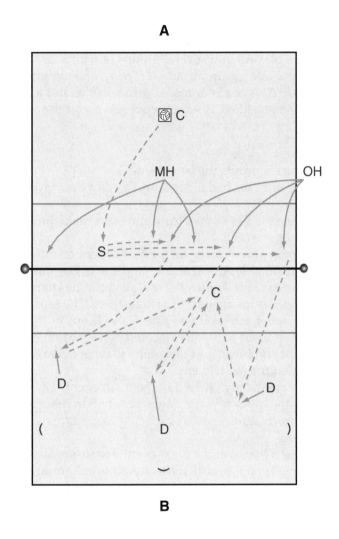

B

Purpose

To allow players to face off in small groups and to encourage competitive play by rewarding winning groups with more competition.

Setup

The coach divides players into several groups of triples or quads. One group starts on side B and one group on side A. The remaining groups wait behind the endline on side A. A coach or tosser with a feeder and a supply of balls is outside the sideline on side B. A scorekeeper sets up off the court, near but not at the net.

Run the Drill

1. The coach tosses or hits the ball to side A.
2. Players rally until the ball is dead, and a point is awarded to the side that won the rally.
3. The group on side B is its own team and stays there throughout the game, even if it loses the rally.
4. If the group on side A loses the rally, it moves to the end of the line of extra players on side A, and the first group in that line moves onto side A. If the team on side A wins the rally, it continues to play.
5. All the side A groups are part of a single team. The scorekeeper keeps the total team score. Each group on side A also keeps its own tally.
6. The round is played to 6 points (scored by the side B group or by *all* the side A groups combined). At this point, players move onto the next competition, called the main event.
7. Side B is automatically entered in the main event. The two groups from side A with the top scores play against side B in the main event. (If only one group from side A scored points, it alone faces side B in the main event.)
8. If side B wins 6 points in the main event first, it remains on side B for the start of the next game, and all the teams on side A are again in competition against side B.
9. If side A wins 6 points first, the group who is on the court when side A wins the final point is declared the winner of the main event, and that group moves to side B for the start of the next game. The group that was on side B moves to the end of the line at the endline on side A.

Coaching Points

- Because it may not take long for a team to score 6 points, to keep players motivated allow all the groups from side A who scored points to play in the main event.
- Enter balls quickly to keep the competition fast paced.

Variation

When running this drill at camp, the camp coaches can be the team on side B to start.

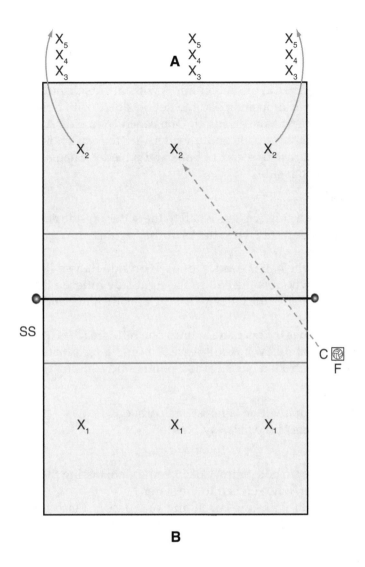

Purpose

To perfect transitional footwork from blocking to hitting and from hitting to blocking.

Setup

A setter is in position 6 at the net on side A with an outside hitter in the left front position. A setter is in position 6 at the net on side B with a right-side hitter in the opposite or right-front position. One coach is on side A in the middle of the court with a cart of balls and a feeder. Another coach is on side B in the middle of the court with a cart of balls and a feeder. Shaggers spread out on the backline on both sides.

Run the Drill

1. The coach on side A tosses a ball to the setter on side A, who sets the ball to the outside hitter, who attacks the ball against the right-side blocker on side B.
2. As soon as the ball is dead, the coach on side B tosses a ball to the setter on side B, who sets the ball to the right-side hitter in the opposite position, who attacks the ball against the outside hitter and left-side blocker on side A.
3. Play continues in this pattern until one hitter reaches 6 points.
4. Scoring is as follows: A kill earns 1 point, a terminating block earns 3 points, a controlled block earns 2 points, and a hitting error loses 1 point.

Coaching Points

- Match up equal hitters against each other.
- Switch setters at the halfway point.

Variations

- Add a passer to both sides. Coaches alternate tossing the ball over the net to the passer, who sends it to the setter.
- Run the drill with one coach and one passer. Place the passer on the opposite side of the net from the coach. The coach tosses the ball to that passer to initiate play on that side and then tosses the ball to the setter on the same side as the coach.

A

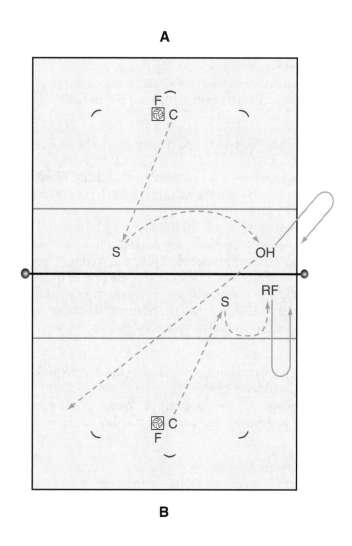

B

Purpose

To introduce a competitive challenge in which all players have to pass, set, and hit by playing doubles with different teammates.

Setup

On two side-by-side courts, a doubles team sets up on each half. Extra players wait at the side and between the courts, ready to rotate into play (see diagram). A coach is at the side of each court with a supply of balls.

Run the Drill

1. A coach enters a free ball to court 1, and the other coach enters a free ball to court 2.
2. The doubles teams on court 1 play out the rally there, and the doubles teams on court 2 play out the rally there. Each player on the winning team of two scores 1 point.
3. Players track their scores individually.
4. After the balls on both courts are played out, everyone rotates one spot counterclockwise and prepares to play the next ball from the coach with a new doubles teammate. For example, the player in the left back goes to the right back. The right-back player rotates off the court to wait to rotate back onto the other side of the net or the other court.
5. Play continues until a player reaches 7 points.

Coaching Points

- Call a score check once in a while during the drill to make sure the players are keeping accurate track of the score.
- Encourage players to be competitive. Watch to see which players adapt easily to the new setup and continue to play hard.

Variations

- Have the players serve.
- Have smaller teams rotate around one court.
- Allow the teams only two contacts.
- Have players rotate after the ball goes over.

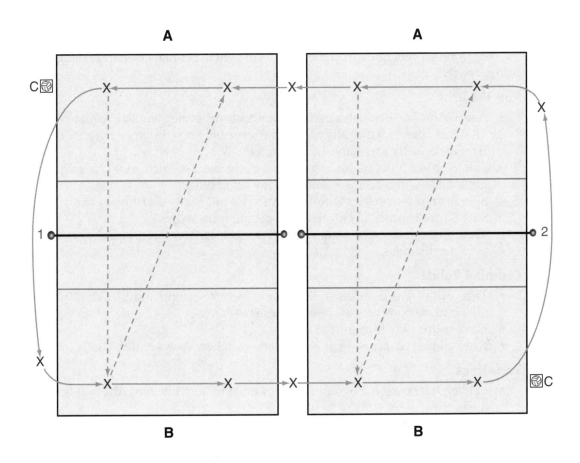

Purpose

To work on scoring from the serve and block, ending the point quickly.

Setup

Balls are placed at the service end of side B. Three blockers set up on side B at the net. Three servers line up on the endline of side B. Six players start on side A in serve receive.

Run the Drill

1. A server on side B initiates play. Servers trade off as they would in a match.
2. The teams play out the rally. Side A can score only by winning a rally. Side B scores only by serve-and-block points.
3. Side B scores 3 points for a service ace or a block, which ends the rally immediately, and scores 1 point for any other block.
4. Side A simply scores by winning a rally. Regular rally scoring applies.
5. Side B tries to score 12 before the opposing team scores 7.
6. Three free missed serves are allowed per game. After three, side A gets a point for the miss.

Coaching Points

- This drill is *fun*! Emphasize the importance of serving and blocking by giving more points for success in these two areas.
- Have teams play three out of five.
- Keep all players active by having them switch sides every three balls.

Variations

- Let beginners score 3 by any block or even by just touching the ball on the block.
- Place an optional defensive specialist and a libero in positions 5 and 6 on side B.
- Let the winning team choose whether to serve and block or to receive.

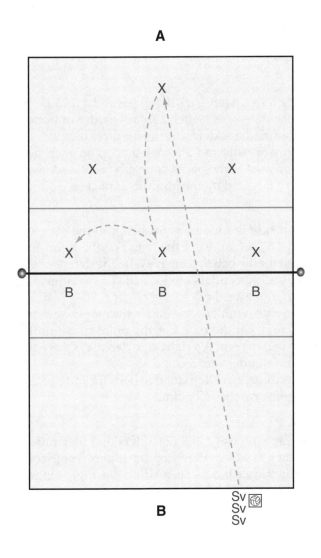

LEFT-SIDE HITTERS VS. MIDDLE HITTER AND OPPOSITES

Purpose

To teach players to hit aggressively against a single block to a specific area of the court; to have outside hitters compete against middle hitters teamed with opposites, with a focus on attacking the line.

Setup

A setter, an outside hitter, a left-back defender, and a middle-back defender set up on side B in base defense. A setter, a middle hitter or opposite, a right-back defender, and a middle-back defender set up on side A in free-ball position. A coach with a supply of balls and a feeder sets up on each side. A scorekeeper is off court, near but not at the net. A cone can be placed near each endline to mark the boundary targeted by the opposing attacker.

Run the Drill

1. The coach on side B initiates a free ball into the players on side A, who attempt to pass, set, and kill the ball. For the point to count, team A's attacker must hit the ball to team B's left-side defense, where the left-back and middle-back defenders are located. The middle attacker hits power or crosscourt, not a cut-back swing or shot.
2. The coach on side A initiates the ball to the player on side B, who attempts to pass, set, and kill the ball. For the point to count, team B's attacker must hit the ball to team A's right-side defense, where the right-back and middle-back defenders are located.
3. The coach continues to alternate free balls for the teams to play out until one of the teams reaches 15 points.

Coaching Points

- Stress defensive intensity. Tell defenders that they must get two touches on the ball they attack so they stop the hitters from scoring.
- Make sure the single blocker is reading the angle of the hitter since play at the net is 1v1.

Variations

- Have players score points by crosscourt kills.
- Use a double-block.

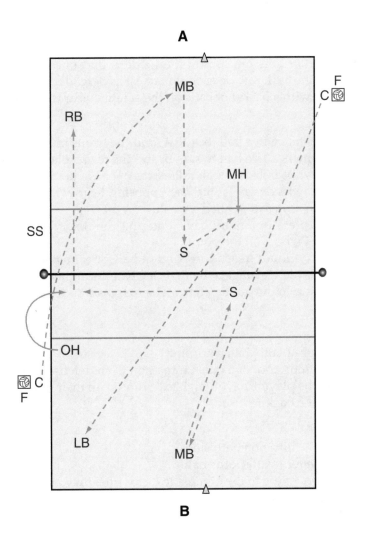

Purpose

To improve ball control and back-row attacking and to practice smooth transitions from defense to offense.

Setup

One front-row setter gets into position on side A and one on side B. Three players set up in the back row on each side to act as defenders and attackers. A coach is off court with a basket of balls on the sideline near the center of court.

Run the Drill

1. The coach enters a free ball to side A, and the teams play out the rally.
2. The coach enters a free ball to side B, and the teams play out the rally.
3. If one team wins both free-ball rallies, they score a point.
4. If one team wins one rally and the opposing team wins the other rally, neither team scores. It's called a wash.
5. The coach enters two more balls, entering the first free ball to side B, regardless of who won the point.
6. The coach continues to send in pairs of balls for the teams to play out, alternating which team gets the first free ball throughout.
7. Play continues in the same pattern. The first team to score 7 points is the winner.

Coaching Points

- Demand high-quality ball control.
- Stress the importance of a quick transition from defense to offense.
- Make sure the players have a high extension with their hitting arm while contacting the back-row set.

Variations

- Add a middle hitter on both sides.
- Allow the setter to attack the ball.
- Make players rotate to the other side every time they attack the ball.
- Disallow tips in front of the 10-foot (3 m) line.

A

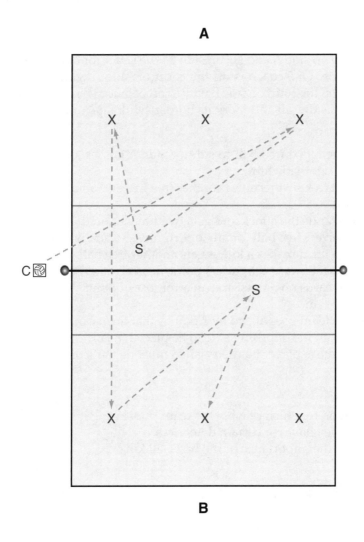

B

Purpose

To give the outside hitters the opportunity to compete against one another in a 6v6 competitive situation.

Setup

Six players set up on side A and six on side B. The setter for both sides is in the right-back position. One coach is off the court on side A with a cart of balls. Another coach is off the court on side B with a cart of balls. The coaches designate an off-court area as the jail and mark its borders with tape or cones.

Run the Drill

1. The coach enters a free ball to side A. Side A passes and sets either the left-side or right-side hitter.
2. If side A gets a kill, it receives another free ball and an opportunity to get another kill.
3. If side B defends the attack and gets two touches on the ball, it is side B's turn to receive a free ball for an opportunity to score on a kill.
4. Each time a team makes a kill, it gets another free ball.
5. Scoring is as follows: A kill earns 1 point, neutral (defense gets two touches on the ball) earns no points, and an error loses 1 point. A team must score 10 points to win.
6. Once either team goes ahead by 2 points, that team can select a back-row defender from the opposing side to be placed in jail.
7. The team whose player has been jailed must tie the score to get its player out of jail.

Coaching Points

- Pay attention to which players the team puts in jail; it shows the respect and trust they have for certain defenders.
- Emphasize the importance of the first-ball kill.

Variation

Allow the team to select a middle blocker to go to jail.

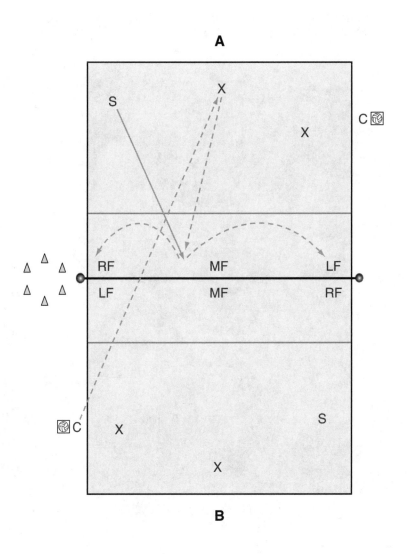

chapter 9

Team Scoring Drills

In every team scoring drill in this chapter, six players compete against six players. The method of entering the ball, the focus of the players and coaches, and the scoring systems vary. Players are assigned roles and given opportunities to improve in those roles. They must perform skills in combination with a full set of teammates against another set of teammates. The games are inviting, team oriented, and highly competitive. Finally, the complete volleyball skill package is demanded.

Team scoring drills work well in midseason and postseason. These drills should not routinely make up the bulk of practice time, but they can on given days. If a team neglects team drills and focuses only on individual and small-group drills, the team may not play well together and may appear disjointed. Team play allows players to develop flow and to work smoothly as a cohesive, coordinated unit. Practicing these drills allows coaches to see what works well, who works well together, and which aspects of the game still need to be worked on in small groups.

Team drills promote player development in leadership, followership, fellowship, decision making, respect, discipline, and more. Quick hand slapping, team yells, encouragement to teammates, and pats on the back are important components of the drills.

You can determine substitutions and assign them before the drill. Specify your expectations regarding substitutions so that the process does not affect the flow of play. Players can substitute quickly after low-scoring games or during games if players know ahead of time who switches with whom and when—after a predetermined number of plays, points, or contacts.

Expect surprises. Expect to stop. Expecting and dealing with the unexpected are what you and your players need to do on game day. Embrace unexpected events, but don't let them derail the practice. Enjoy victories. Be as specific as possible with your instructions. Keep your corrections, suggestions, and comments brief and to the point. Conditions should be as gamelike as possible during team scoring drills.

Team drills facilitate team cohesion, team will and drive, and an intense competitiveness. Keep the scoring system low so players can experience the thrill of winning more often.

It is not necessary to play to 25 every time your team plays a competition at practice, but it is necessary to do it sometimes. Mostly, create short games. Then, in true matches, remind them to break the long game of 25 points into smaller, attainable goals.

It is also important to play games in practice that allow players to learn to handle gamelike scores, such as 23 to 24 or 24 to 23. Give players the chance to play the underdog and fight to come back and win. Let them also learn to feel comfortable moving from a 1-point lead to a solid victory. You can put these experiences in your pocket and remind your players when this happens in a game that the situation is not unique and they've faced it before. Rehearsing circumstances like these in practice reduces the stress when they occur in matches.

The most important reason for doing 6v6 drills in practice is to provide match-day opportunities for players. This type of drill is the dress rehearsal for matches. Remember to address match-day details such as lineups, changing of sides, substitution rules, ball shagging, and so on. Every issue you must deal with in a contest should be addressed. If everything is well rehearsed, players are comfortable on match day. It is then a fun day of competition rather than a stress-filled, stomach-churning nightmare. Not surprisingly, if the team is well rehearsed, the coach is also more comfortable during the event and can better respond to the needs of the team as the match progresses. Team scoring drills are winning opportunities for all involved.

Purpose

To establish control of the pass, set, and attack and end with a termination.

Setup

Six players set up on each side of the net, with players on both team A and team B in their specialized positions. One coach is on the sideline of side A with a basket of balls. Another coach is on the sideline on side B with a basket of balls.

Run the Drill

1. The coach on side A sends a free ball to the team on side B, who must pass, set, and attack the ball.
2. Every time the ball crosses the net, both teams and subs yell out the next letter in the word rally: R-A-L-L-Y.
3. Once the last letter is called and the full word had been spelled out, the teams attempt to terminate the ball.
4. The team that errs or does not win the point receives the next free ball from the coach on the opposite side of the net.
5. Each termination scores a point. The first team to 7 points wins.

Coaching Points

- Be sure that all players call out the letters; this will promote communication and loud vocal calls.
- Insist on 3-option passes so they are able to run in system.
- Communicate with your hitters throughout the drill. Let them know when they should go for the termination or keep the attack in play.

Variation

For less experienced teams, change the word to *win*.

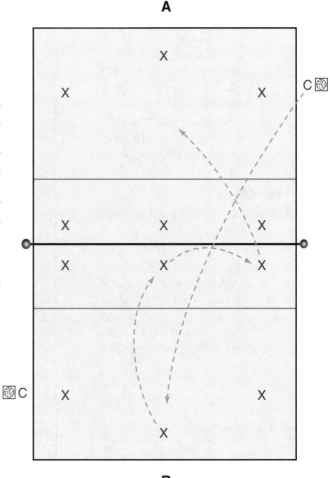

GOLDEN BALL

Purpose

To provide a gamelike competition with the added pressure and joy of a bonus ball and decision-making opportunity.

Setup

Two teams of six set up on opposites sides of the court. Substitutes are predetermined. A coach and basket of balls are at the side of the court. A scorekeeper is on the sideline near the net.

Run the Drill

1. The coach enters the ball by tossing or hitting to either side.
2. The team that wins the rally gets 1 point, and the coach tosses in another ball.
3. Teams play to 15 points.
4. At a point in the drill of the coach's choosing, the coach tosses in the golden ball, which is a different color or specially marked. The winner of the golden-ball rally can alter the score by declaring it tied or by awarding themselves 3 points, whichever they prefer.

Coaching Points

- Use this drill to equalize the odds in a competition between the starting lineup and players with less experience or other mismatched groups.
- Purchase a gold-colored volleyball to give players the fun of playing with the "real thing."

Variations

- Break out the golden ball during any drill at any time to shake up the scoring.
- If the team scores a quick attack (or some other designated task) when the golden ball is in play, that team wins the game.

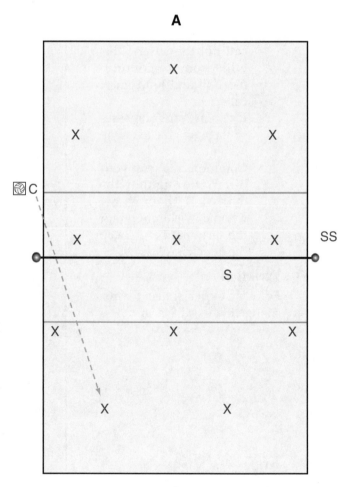

ROTATION RACE

This is a 6v6 serve-receive contest.

Purpose

To practice serve-receive patterns in all rotations.

Setup

Six players set up on each side of the court. Side A always receives. Side B always serves. A basket of balls is on the endline of side B. If there are more than 12 players, the coach preassigns substitutions.

Run the Drill

1. Side B serves to side A.
2. Players rally until the ball is dead.
3. The winner of the rally receives 1 point.
4. Side A (receiving team) must score 2 points in each rotation.
5. The serving team tries to score 12 before the opponent scores 15.
6. Side B does not rotate. The three back-row players alternate serving.
7. The serving team is allowed three missed serves, then side A scores a point for each missed serve. This encourages aggressive serving.
8. The winning team can choose to serve or receive the following game.

Coaching Points

- For a beginning team, keep serve-receive positioning simple, but start letting primary passers into key positions.
- Use this opportunity to discuss overlapping.

Variations

- Award a bonus point for scoring on a first attack for the receiving team and rotate automatically.
- Award a bonus point for an ace.

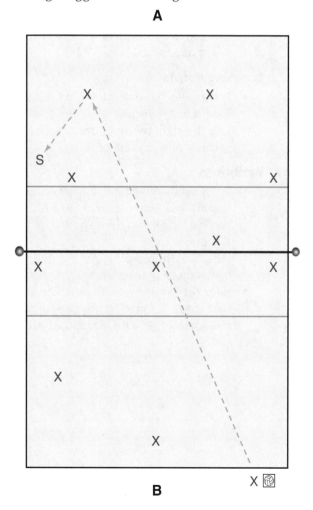

BASEBALL

Purpose

To provide a fun and competitive 6v6 drill with a scoring system from a different sport.

Setup

Six players set up on side A and six players on side B. A cart of balls is on each endline. Assign substitutes to positions before starting the game.

Run the Drill

1. Side A serves to side B. The serving team represents the team in the field in baseball terms.
2. Side B receives the serve. The receiving team represents the batting team in baseball terms and is trying to score *runs* by siding out.
3. Teams play out the rally. If side A wins, it makes an *out*. Its goal is to make three outs so that it can come *up to bat*.
4. If side B wins the rally, it scores a point, like scoring a run. For each rally it wins while representing the batting team, it scores a point.
5. Once side A has made three outs while in the field (won three rallies while serving), it gets the chance to bat, or serve receive.
6. The coach substitutes players on both teams only on an out.
7. Scoring is cumulative for the entire game of five to seven innings or as many as time allows.

Coaching Points

- It helps to have someone who just keeps score. It's fun to do this on a baseball-style scorebook, but you can improvise on a dry-erase board.
- Use this drill for an entire practice or play only a few *innings*, depending on how players respond.

Variations

- Advanced: When side B receives serve, count that as a *hit* and side B now has an imaginary runner on first. Another hit puts runners on first and second, and so on. If the bases are loaded and side B gets another hit, side B scores a run.
- Add the double play: An ace or a stuff block by the serving team counts as two *outs* against the team at bat.
- Add the home run: An attacked ball by the team *at bat* (receiving team) that lands directly on the floor of the serving team before anyone touches it is a homerun! This clears the bases, scoring every runner who is on base.

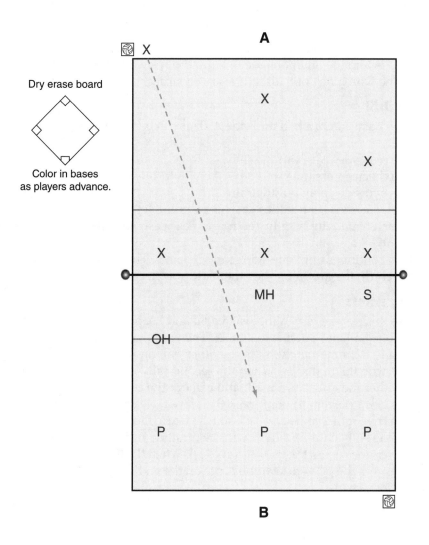

A

Dry erase board

Color in bases
as players advance.

X

X

X

X X X

MH S

OH

P P P

B

Purpose

To encourage teams to focus on both offense and defense in order to be successful.

Setup

The coach divides players into groups of three plus one setter. One group sets up on side A and the other on side B. Extra groups wait off court. A coach is on the sideline with a cart of balls and a scoreboard.

Run the Drill

1. The coach enters a ball into side A. This can be a serve, down ball, or free ball.
2. The two sides play out the rally.
3. The coach enters the same type of ball into side B that was sent to side A.
4. The two sides play out the rally.
5. If a team wins both rallies, it scores a point.
6. If each team wins a rally, the round is a wash and neither team scores a point.
7. Play continues until one side scores 3 points. The winning group stays on the court; the group on the other side is replaced.

Coaching Points

- Use this system to run the wash drill and keep the scoring straight: Pick up one ball and enter it to side A. Then pick up two balls and enter one to side B. Immediately place the other ball on the same side as the team that won the first rally. When the second rally is over, quickly determine whether the round is a wash and call out the correct score.
- Use extra players to help track the score for each side. Each time side A wins two rallies and scores a point, an extra player lines up on the endline of side A. Each time side B wins two rallies and scores a point, an extra player lines up on the endline of side B. When the third and winning point is scored, the players keeping score on the endline replace the players on the losing side.

Variations

- Use groups of two, four, or five.
- Use wash scoring for many of the drills throughout the book.

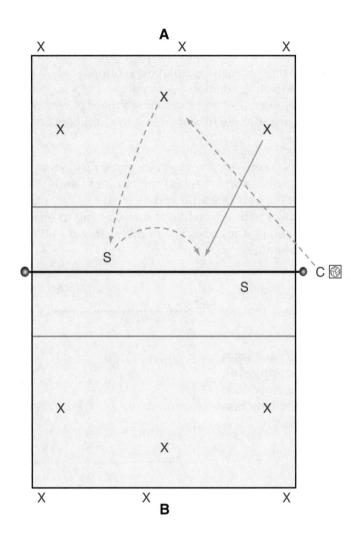

This game helps the team to play hard for every point.

Purpose

To improve focus at the start of the set and throughout the entire set.

Setup

Six players set up on side A and six players set up on side B in their respective serve and receive starting rotations. A supply of balls is on each endline. The coach prepares a brown paper bag containing slips of papers with numbers from 1 to 25. The slips of paper are folded so that the numbers are hidden.

Run the Drill

1. The captains meet with the coach off the court before play begins, and one player picks a number out of the bag and hands it to the coach.
2. The coach is the only one who knows what number was picked.
3. Teams compete with normal volleyball scoring in effect until one team reaches a score that matches the number drawn at the start of the drill and wins the game.

Coaching Point

Encourage players to play each point as if it were the last.

Variation

Tell one player on each team what score they are playing to. Watch to see how that player handles the situation and how she or he may lead.

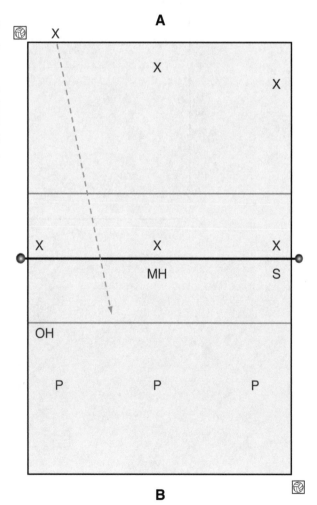

Purpose

To emphasize and improve a particular skill during a set.

Setup

The coach creates a golden ticket out of sturdy colored paper. Six players set up on side A and six players set up on side B in their respective serve and receive starting rotations. A supply of balls is on each endline.

Run the Drill

1. The coach announces a skill that players must perform in order to earn the golden ticket.
2. Teams compete, with normal volleyball scoring in effect.
3. If a team performs the specified skill and wins the golden ticket, it can swap scores with its opponent at any time. Team members can strategize to determine the best time to redeem the ticket. To redeem it, they return the ticket to the coach.
4. However, the opponent can win back the golden ticket by completing the skill before it is used to switch scores. This too is a point of strategy.
5. The first team to score 15 points wins.

Coaching Points

- Choose a skill you want your team to focus on throughout the set as the skill that earns the golden ticket. Possibilities include a solo block that results in a point, a middle attack such as a slide that results in a kill, an ace serve, and a back-row attack that results in a kill.
- Winning the golden ticket should be difficult so that the golden ticket is not exchanged too often. Frequent exchanges alter the natural flow of the game.

Variations

- Make the golden ticket worth 2 or 5 points that can be added to the team's score or deducted from the opponent's score.
- Increase the score needed to win the set to 25 points.

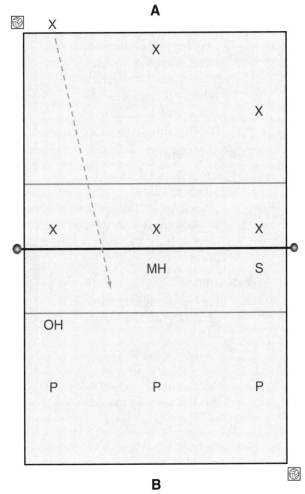

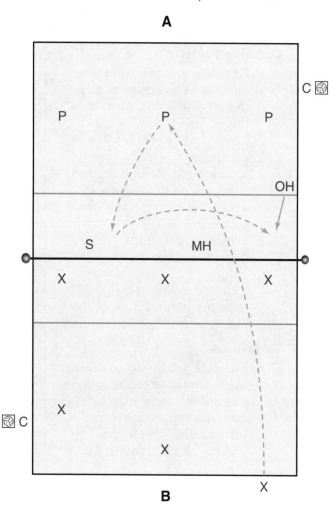

FOUR-BALL WASH

Purpose

To create intense 6v6 competition by using a variety of entered balls.

Setup

Six players set up on side A and on side B. The coach decides the rotation. One coach is on side A outside the court, and another coach is on side B outside the court. Each coach has a supply of balls.

Run the Drill

1. Side A starts in serve receive.
2. Side B starts in defense.
3. Side B serves to side A, and the ball is played out.
4. The coach on side A then enters two consecutive down balls to side B, one at a time, and the teams play out the rallies. The teams keep track of how many rallies they win.
5. The coach on side B then enters a free ball into side A and it is played out.
6. At the end of the four-ball sequence, if both sides have each won two rallies, no points are awarded. If one side has won three rallies, it is awarded 1 point. If one side has won all four rallies, it is awarded 2 points.
7. Play continues until one team earns 5 points. Continuously alternate which team gets the serve and free balls or the two down balls.

Coaching Points

- Insist on total focus for all four rallies.
- Encourage players to be patient. It may take a long time to score 5 points.

Variations

- Play in a single rotation or rotate after a series of balls.
- Increase or decrease the number of points needed to win, based on the amount of time you want to play.

Purpose

To improve side-out consistency.

Setup

Six players set up on side A in serve-receive offense. Six players set up on side B in defense ready to serve. A supply of balls is on each endline. A coach with a whistle is on the sideline.

Run the Drill

1. Side B serves to side A, and the ball is played out.
2. Side A must win three out of five serves to move to the next rotation.
3. As soon as side A is unable to win at least three out of five serves, it becomes side B's opportunity to receive the serve.
4. As soon as a team wins three out of the five, it moves to its next rotation.
5. The first team to get through all six rotations wins.

Coaching Points

- As soon as a team gets three side-outs, rotate, even if five serves aren't necessary for success.
- Start in your weakest rotation.

Variations

- To win the game, a team must rotate through all six rotations twice.
- Have just one side receive the serves and put a time limit on the drill.

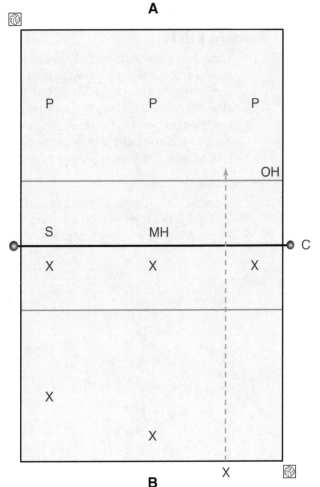

Purpose

To provide an opportunity to improve the accuracy of the pass, thus providing greater opportunity for first-ball kills by the attacker.

Setup

Six players get into serve-receive position on side A. Six players set up on side B on defense with a server prepared to serve. A cart of balls is near the endline on both sides.

Run the Drill

1. Team B serves to team A.
2. Team A attempts to pass a 3 ball (ball that gives the setter the option of setting any one of the three hitters) and terminate a first-ball kill.
3. If team A passes a 3 ball and terminates a first-ball kill, the team gets a point.
4. If team A does not pass a 3 ball that results in a first-ball kill but still wins the rally, team A retains the opportunity to serve receive.
5. If team B wins the rally, team B has the opportunity to serve receive and score a point with a three-option pass that results in a first-ball kill.
6. The first team to 11 points wins.

Coaching Points

- This drill puts tremendous pressure on the passer to consistently pass three-option balls. Emphasize to your players that passing consistency is a must for winning this drill, but remind them to have short memories after an error. Insist on fast mental recoveries.
- Point out to players that they must trust one another to be successful. The back row must trust the front row, and the front row must trust the back row in order to score points.

Variations

- Increase or decrease the number of points necessary to win the game.
- Make a specific hit worth 2 points, such as a middle attack.
- Players love the opportunity to compete with coaches.

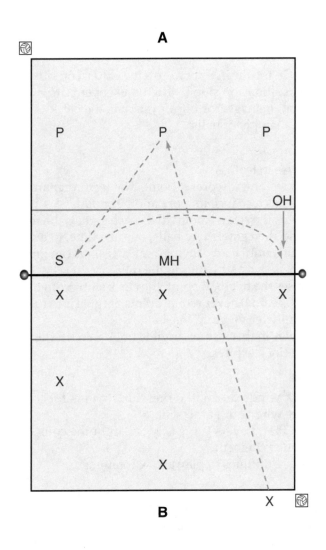

This is a high-energy, high-intensity drill.

Purpose

To provide an intense 6v6 game focused on serve receive and free balls.

Setup

Six players set up in the desired serve-receive pattern on side A. Six players set up in defensive positions on side B. The timekeeper puts two minutes on the clock. An assistant, manager, or off-player runs the clock. A coach sets up on the sideline with a supply of balls.

Run the Drill

1. Team B serves to team A.
2. If team A sides-out, it scores a point. The team prepares to serve receive again and gains a chance to score another point.
3. If team B wins the service point, the coach signals the timekeeper to start the clock and then enters free balls, one at a time, to team B.
4. The clock runs until team A wins a rally. Team A can only score points by receiving the serve and winning the rally.
5. If team B loses the free-ball point, the clock stops with the remaining time on the clock. Team B never scores points; its goal is to run the clock to zero by successfully terminating free balls.
6. Play continues in this fashion until team A scores 6 side-out points or the time on the clock expires.

Coaching Points

- As the clock winds down, the pressure mounts for the receiving team. Watch to see who your gamers are.
- Use a clock that players can easily see from the court. This adds to the pressure and excitement.
- It takes just 12 minutes to play all six rotations.

Variations

- Increase or decrease the number of points team A needs to score to win the game according to the team's level.
- Increase the amount of time on the clock that team B must expire to win the game.

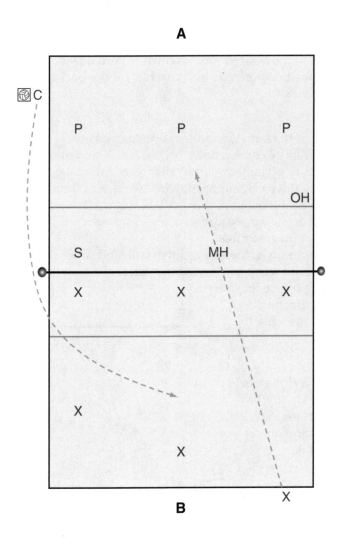

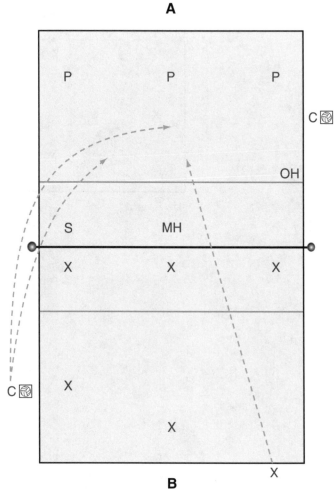

Purpose

To allow players to work on offensive play by receiving three consecutive balls: a serve, a down ball, and a free ball.

Setup

Six players set up in the desired serve-receive pattern on side A. Six players set up in defensive positions on side B. A coach is off the backcourt on each side with a supply of balls.

Run the Drill

1. Team B serves to team A, and the rally is played out.
2. The coach on side B enters a down ball to team A, and the rally is played out.
3. The coach on side B initiates a free ball to team A, and the rally is played out.
4. If team A, as the receiving team, wins two out of three rallies, it earns 1 point. If it wins three out of three rallies, it earns 2 points.
5. The team on defense does not win points. That team's objective is to prevent the opponent from scoring.
6. Team B now receives the serve, down ball, and free ball and attempts to earn points. The scoring system is the same.
7. Teams rotate before they serve.
8. Continue alternating until one team wins 15 points.

Coaching Point

Enter the balls at a slower or quicker pace to vary the difficulty to suit the team's level. The pace should be challenging but manageable.

Variations

- Play the game to fewer points to make the game faster.
- Require the receiving team to win all three balls to win a point.
- Have a coach serve the ball instead of the players to eliminate service errors or to focus on a certain passer or rotation.
- Allow the defensive side to score a point for each ball it wins.

BONGO

Purpose

To emphasize the importance of siding-out consistently and to place a high value on a scored serving point.

Setup

Six players set up in defensive positions on side A. Six players set up in the desired serve-receive pattern on side B. A supply of balls is at each endline.

Run the Drill

1. Team A serves at team B.
2. Team B attempts to earn one big point by winning three side-out points in a row to then rotate and have an opportunity to serve for a point.
3. When team A successfully defends its serve, it has the opportunity to serve receive.
4. Team B serves to team A, who attempts to side-out three times in a row in order to rotate and have an opportunity to serve for a big point.
5. Whenever a team does not successfully serve receive and side-out three times in a row, it is the opposing team's opportunity to serve receive.
6. The first team to reach 5 points is the winner.

Coaching Points

- It is extremely difficult to score a point, so errors are magnified. Stress the importance of focusing for all four rallies: three successful side-outs and 1 served point.
- Watch to see how players stand up to the pressure. This drill places major pressure on the server once the server's team successfully sides-out three times in a row.

Variations

- Decrease the number of points required to win the game.
- Decrease the number of side-outs required from three to two.

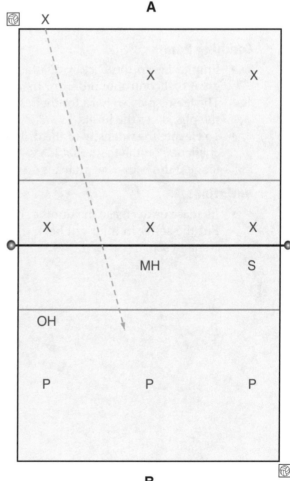

Purpose

To prepare one player to become the primary back-row attacker.

Setup

Six players set up in a defensive position on both sides of the net. The primary attacker is in the middle-back position. A coach with a basket of balls is on the sideline near the center of the court on both sides of the net.

Run the Drill

1. The coach on side A enters a free ball to side B, and the teams play the ball out. Only the designated back-row attacker is allowed to aggressively go for a kill. Other players must tip or roll-shot the ball into play.
2. The coach on side B enters a free ball to side A, and the teams play the ball out. Only the designated back-row attacker is allow to aggressively go for a kill. Other players must tip or roll-shot the ball into play.
3. If one team wins both free-ball rallies, it scores a point.
4. If one team wins one rally and the opposing team wins the other rally, neither team scores a point—this is called a wash.
5. The coach enters a free ball to side B next no matter who won the first point. The coach alternates which team gets the first free ball throughout the drill.
6. The drill continues in the same pattern until one side gets 4 points.

Coaching Points

- Emphasize to the back-row attacker's teammates that they must have great ball control in order for their back-row teammate to win this drill. The teams play so hard for their designated attacker that the drill pushes the players to the limit.
- To elevate the intensity of the drill, put a consequence such as a physical challenge on the team that loses. The teammates must perform the challenge if the back-row attacker does not win the drill.

Variations

- Increase or decrease the number of points needed to win the game.
- Put the setter in the right back so that the right-front player must occasionally set.

A

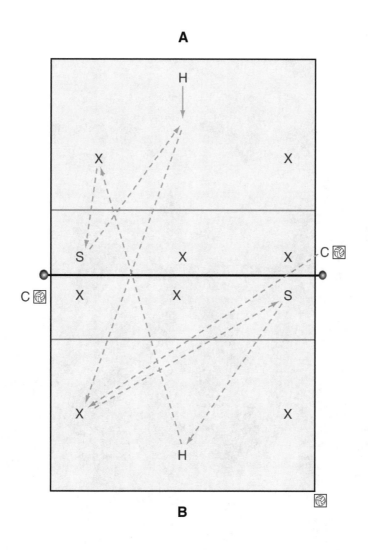

B

chapter 10

Mental-Toughness and Team-Building Drills

Because time in the gym and during contests is limited, we strongly encourage you to take time for team development through off-court activities. The connections between players and between coaches and players are important. Remember, this desire to connect with others is the reason many athletes choose team sports over individual sports. Although the love of the sport is a factor, it would be incorrect to assume that this alone drives all players to commit to volleyball.

All team activities, whether they include social gatherings, meals, movies, or other events are opportunities for athletes to get to know each other better. Getting to know where each player comes from, learning about their families, wishes, and desires, and finding out why they play the sport and generally what makes them tick are important. It helps players understand themselves and each other better. This self-knowledge and understanding of other players make for better communication within the team. Players are different, and we ask them to come together with people they might never have met otherwise and play as one in a sport that they may not even know well. Volleyball will be the common bond between them. Off-court activities help to connect them emotionally. Having fun together creates a will to work together in the gym at practice and to achieve together.

As a coach, you must ask yourself some questions about your coaching philosophy and the type of team you wish to have. The answers to these questions serve as a guide to your behavior and the expectations you have of your players.

What personality do you want your team to have and how should that personality be expressed?

What kind of coach do you want to be? Cooperative? Commanding? Demanding?

Do you listen? Do you learn? Do you show respect to your players?

Do players listen? Do players learn? Do players show respect to you and to each other?

Do players want to be around you and around each other?

Is your gym an inviting place to be? Is fun encouraged? Can hard work and fun and laughter coexist?

Players may not have given much thought to their personal philosophies. It is your responsibility as a coach to help players develop mentally and emotionally as well as physically. Just as you teach the physical skills they need, you must also challenge them to develop the mental and emotional strength to succeed.

This chapter invites you and your players to explore these questions and to learn about each other. It encourages you and your players to examine your behavior and its consequences, your goals, your attitudes about competition and leadership, and what it takes to be part of a winning program. It offers activities you can use to initiate, implement, or enhance the bond and the mindset of a united, competitive team.

Let other programs wonder whether you win because you have fun or have fun because you win!

Coaches and others often debate whether athletes are born competitive or they learn to be competitive. Try this: Start incorporating conversations about competition with your team. Be excited about victories, even small ones that occur daily, talk about competition, and be competitive yourself. Then answer whether a player's competitive spirit can be influenced. Players who want to contribute to a team that they have grown attached to and have a common bond with, who are offered competitive opportunities and are encouraged to make the most of them, and who experience winning on and off the court will want to win more.

Be creative, Coach! Adapt the activities in this chapter as you need to for your team. Create moments that are decidedly owned by your team. A sharing circle or happy huddle that starts practice with positive sharing takes a moment or two but is like connective tissue. It helps hold the team together. In the same way a uniform identifies a team, shared activities, outings, and discussions; bows or signs; locker room or bulletin board messages; and quotes, songs, and cheers identify players as part of a special group. Celebrate what is unique about your team. Help players identify the common goals that bring them together this season. Do everything you can as a coach to help players succeed.

A unique team song may annoy other teams, crack players up every time they hear it, and make opponents envy your spirit!

Purpose

To encourage interaction, teamwork, creativity, fun, and development of a team song.

Setup

The coach names a leader from team members for the activity. Creativity helps, so coaches can ask players to choose a *creative leader*.

Run the Drill

1. The team decides on a childhood or well-known tune to use for the team song. "Yankee Doodle Dandy," "When the Saints Go Marching In," and similar tunes work well.
2. Players make up lyrics for the song; however, there is a theme: teamwork!
3. Players must use the following words in the song:

   Spirit
   Team
   Friend
   Winner
   Whiner
   Ding

Coaching Point

Choose a set of words that have particular meaning to your players. Adding a unique or funny word adds humor.

Variation

Choose an alternative theme for the song: the name of the school team, name of the school, and so on.

CHAIN STORY

Purpose

To foster open communication, help teammates bond, and create laughter and fun.

Setup

The coaches and players sit in a circle. The coach assigns the name of a fictional team to be used in the chain story. If the team is large, the coach can break the team into small groups.

Run the Drill

1. The coach announces that the challenge is to create a story about a high school volleyball team that started the season with no success off the court or on the court, until suddenly something changed.
2. Starting with the coach and moving clockwise around the circle, each player provides one sentence in the story.
3. As the activity continues, players craft a story that tells how, where, and why things changed for the team.

Coaching Point

Encourage players to be creative and have fun with this activity, but also to think it through logically and thoughtfully.

Variation

Tell the story in reverse. The team is doing well until something happens (a new player is negative or critical, the team loses a big game and players blame each other) and then they begin to struggle. Finish by circling back to how the team turned the setback around.

BULLETIN BOARD

Purpose

To give players the opportunity to create and use an information and learning center for the team.

Setup

The coach designates or provides a board, wall, or other space for sharing information, inspiration, and ideas. The coach can provide or ask players to provide materials such as colored paper, stencils, tape, stapler, and so on. These can be left in a place where players can access them to update the board.

Run the Drill

1. The coach develops a "Coach's Corner" or special area of the board to post schedules, practice times, holiday break information, and so on.
2. To get players involved, the coach can brainstorm with players about other things to post. The coach and players can even draw out the bulletin board on paper or a poster and assign sections for various topics.
3. Each player's name and number should be on the board somewhere. A special section could be updated by a different team member each week. Or players could each be responsible for one aspect of updating the board: one player posts an item of interest from the school or local paper, another contributes a drawing or quote, and so on.

Coaching Points

- Make the board a priority right from the start of the season. Assign each player a role in creating or updating the board.
- Use pictures of the coaches and team members. Baby pictures are fun.
- Include names of new volleyball books or articles to read.
- Create a section for a question of the week where players can post their answers. Each week ask them to name their favorite food, color, movie, athlete, team, and so on.

Variation

Create a team website.

I WAS WONDERING

Purpose

To address, at the beginning of a new season, preparation concerns so that players can be more organized and well prepared.

Setup

Provide players with slips of paper and pens or pencils.

Run the Drill

1. Each player writes down a question that relates to volleyball preparedness, training, or time management.
2. Some questions may be player centered, such as the following:
   Why is Kyle always on time?
   Why is Mary always so pulled together with her practice clothes?
   How does Courtney find time to lift weights every day?
   Where does Joe get his shoes?
   The player mentioned in the question can answer it.
3. Other more general questions may arise, such as the following:
   What should go into a workout bag? How should it be organized, and when should it be packed?
   What kind of kneepads and shoes are best?
   How do players balance volleyball, school, and socializing?
   The players can answer these questions as a group, so that they can compare notes and share tips.
4. The coach can raise questions that players might not think to ask, such as the following:
   What should players eat?
   How much water do players need to drink?
   Are players having trouble finding time to study? Anyone need a tutor?
   Is transportation difficult? Might players want to carpool?

Coaching Points

- Besides generating helpful information about volleyball concerns, these question and answer sessions encourage players to share, trust, and help each other. Remind players that they can turn to each other for answers and for help—and that when they do, they strengthen the team.
- Encourage players to stand up for each other. Players should know that whatever anyone else might do or say, the team is there to support them.

Variation

Instead of writing a question, each player completes the sentence, "When I was first starting out in volleyball, I wish someone had told me . . ."

I AM COMPETITIVE

Purpose

To encourage all players to develop the belief in themselves that they, too, can be more competitive, regardless of their makeup.

Setup

The coach and players sit in a tight circle. A white board or poster board and markers are in the middle of the circle. The coach asks a player to read the following statements to the team:

>*A player with a loud personality can be competitive.*
>
>*A player with a quiet, soft personality can be competitive.*
>
>*A tall player can be competitive.*
>
>*A short player can be competitive.*
>
>*A person who is terminally ill can be competitive.*
>
>*A player who plays Beethoven on the piano can be competitive.*
>
>*A person with no tan can be competitive.*
>
>*A person who doesn't clean his or her room can be competitive.*
>
>*A person with no legs can be competitive.*
>
>*A player who loves physics can be competitive.*
>
>*A person who can't swim can be competitive.*

Run the Drill

1. The coach poses questions for discussion:
   So what makes someone competitive?
   Are some people born competitive?
2. Players contribute freely to the discussion and compare their thoughts on this with each other. There are no right or wrong answers.
3. Team members share their personal experiences. The coach asks players who are willing to participate to complete these statements in front of the team:
   I am competitive because _____.
   I need to _____ to become more competitive.
4. The coach asks players to fill in the blank in the following sentence. As responses are offered, the coach or players write them on the board.
   We need to _____ to be more competitive.

Coaching Points

- Emphasize the following as you wrap up the discussion:
  People *can* learn to be more competitive.
  Watch and study competitive people. Learn from them.
  Keep score with yourself. For example, see how many sets you can make in a row or how fast you can run a mile (1.6 km).
  Keep score with others. Competing makes you compete better.
  Remember the feeling every time you win . . . at anything. It is the *feeling* that you want to repeat. It is not really the score. You want to get that feeling again!
- Give players as many opportunities as possible for repetitions, and encourage them to do them on their own. A player can never repeat too many passes, serves, and other skills. When a skill comes naturally, players can focus more on competing and less on the skills.
- Play a ton of triples and doubles so players get repetitions and the chance to compete.

WHATEVER

Purpose

To encourage an understanding of positive communication, both verbal and nonverbal, when dealing with those in a position of authority.

Setup

The coach divides the team into two groups. Each group sits in a line facing the other. Each person in group A assumes the role of a person in an authoritative position, such as a parent, principal, policeman, coach, or teacher. The coach can assign the roles, players can provide suggestions, or each member of the group can choose a position of authority. Each person in group B assumes the role of someone who is expected to take direction from the person across from her or him. For example, if the first person in group A assumes the role of a teacher, the first person group B assumes the role of a student.

Run the Drill

1. One at a time each member of group A, in the position of authority, makes a statement to the teammate directly across from her or him in group B. The statement should be something a person with that role would be likely to say. Players can be creative and make up a situation they have not been a part of, such as a famous director giving notes to an actor, or they can use a cliché such as a parent saying, "Get right back in here and clean your room."
2. Each person in group B responds to the statement from the opposite person with just one word, "Whatever." Group B members can use any facial expressions, body language, and tone of voice they like, but they may only use the word whatever.
3. This continues for a few rounds. The coach will know when enough is enough.
4. Group A members then describe their feelings and reactions to the "Whatever" statement. They may say that it was hurtful or seemed like a brush-off.

Coaching Points

- Ask if there are other under-the-breath dismissive or hurtful comments people often use, and steer the conversation toward the effects of these statements. Talk about how such remarks can be disrespectful, cause people to judge the speaker, lower the speaker's standing in the group, disrupt practice, and more.
- Discuss and encourage the positive characteristics each team member should show during practice. Discuss what to do when one agrees or disagrees with a coaching decision or direction, and how this might affect the team.

HAMMER

"He that is good with a hammer tends to think everything is a nail."

— Anonymous

Purpose

To help players understand the need to touch the volleyball during practice and in matches by discussing and emphasizing the need for repetition.

Setup

The coach reads the following selection to the team before a day of repetition skills or simply to help the team understand the need for repetition.

> When someone in the sport of volleyball hits the ball hard, we often refer to that person as a hammer. When that hammer gets better and better, she or he wants the ball, wants to hit, and will hit any ball. The hammer doesn't care if the set is a bit off, doesn't care if the lights are dim, doesn't find fault with others. The hammer just wants the ball set to her or him and to swing hard at it. It is like the quote. The hammer just wants to hit everything. The ball is the nail! Hit it hard.
>
> We have to think like this in volleyball. Good players want to be the hammer. They want the ball. They want the ball when the game is on the line.
>
> A hammer doesn't have to really be a hitter. A setter can want the ball more than anyone else. A passer can want it more. A libero can want to dig more than a hitter wants to hit.
>
> The team needs players who want the ball! Do you? Do you want it repeatedly so that you can continue to improve and to achieve?
>
> This is why repetitions are so important. The more you set, the better you set. The better you set, the more you are challenged with tougher sets. This means more repetitions. Nothing in volleyball is more important than repetitions.
>
> The more you repeat, the more comfortable you are with the skill. Then in games you are relaxed. You may fall into the zone—the place where you seem to play flawlessly, where it looks easy even when it is hard. This is where you want to be. You can't get there unless skills seem natural to you.

Run the Drill

1. The coach leads a discussion about the reading, highlighting the need for repetitions in volleyball and the need to maintain focus during repetition drills.
2. The coach asks players for input about how to keep players focused. This may vary with the player. The coach and players offer ideas on how to keep busy and active during repetition drills. They explore how to be helpful to teammates during repetition drills.

Coaching Point

During practice and games, remind players of this discussion by telling them to be the hammer! That simple phrase will bring the key points of this activity back to them and keep them motivated.

TEAM CHALLENGE

Purpose

To encourage the team to come up with a plan for change when things become stagnant on or off the court.

Setup

The coach determines when the team needs an extra challenge. This might be indicated when some or all of the players are slow or dragging, low on spirit, not hitting well, feeling crabby and argumentative, or worst of all *whining*! At this point, the coach gathers the team to stand or sit in a circle.

Run the Drill

1. The coach tells players, "It is time to challenge yourselves as a team."
2. The coach asks players to name three issues that the team needs to change . . . and fast! The coach reminds them that everyone can improve and encourages them to be honest with themselves.
3. The team decides on a change or changes that can take place immediately to make a difference. Players challenge themselves to implement the change immediately.

Coaching Points

- Emphasize the need to address problems immediately. Tell players, "Nip it in the bud!" Don't let it worsen. When a problem starts or when a skill is failing *change* is needed.
- Follow up after the next practice or match. Ask players to evaluate whether they changed as a team, whether everyone participated, whether something else needs to be done. If the problem has not been fully resolved, challenge players to find a way to fix it and to demand of themselves that they get it done. Evaluate and reevaluate.

YOU WANT; THEY WANT

If time permits, follow this activity with You Got Game.

Purpose

To reflect on the influence of veteran players on younger, less experienced players.

Setup

The entire team sits in a circle. The coach reads the following, indicating that it is addressed to the team leaders or the seniors.

> *You dream; they dream.*
>
> *You're passionate; they're passionate.*
>
> *You care; they care.*
>
> *You sweat; they sweat.*
>
> *You laugh; they laugh.*
>
> *You cry; they cry.*
>
> *You cheer, they cheer.*
>
> *You love; they love.*
>
> *You give; they give.*
>
> *You give up; they give up.*
>
> *You whine; they whine.*
>
> *You win; they win.*

Run the Drill

1. The coach leads a group discussion, asking the younger, less experienced players the following questions:
   What do you need from senior players?
   What do you notice in senior players?
   What excites you? What fears do you bring with you?
2. Players respond.
3. The coach asks the veteran or senior players the following questions:
   What do you wish for the younger players?
   What is your responsibility to the younger players?
   What do you most want younger players to learn from you?
   What do you each have to offer younger players?
4. Players respond.

Coaching Point

Set a comfortable tone and encourage players in both groups to speak freely and from the heart.

YOU GOT GAME?

Purpose

To reflect on what can be learned by taking the lead of more experienced players.

Setup

The team sits in a circle. The coach reads the following, indicating that it is addressed to rookie or young players on the team.

Earn their respect.

Watch them; learn from them.

Honor their play; honor their soul.

Stand by them; cheer for them.

Praise them; play with them.

Laugh with them; cry with them.

Love them—and take their positions as soon as you can grab them!

Run the Drill

1. The coach leads a discussion of the reading. The coach asks the rookies the following questions:
   What can you do to learn from experienced players?
   How do you let experienced players know that you will willingly and whole-heartedly follow their lead?
   What do you gain by recognizing experienced players?
2. Rookie players respond.
3. The coach asks the veterans the following questions:
   Do you recognize that you are being followed? If so, how do you know?
   Do you feel pressured to set an example? Is it an honor to set an example?
   How can you improve communication with younger players?
4. Veteran players respond.

Coaching Point

Set a comfortable tone and encourage players in both groups to speak freely and from the heart.

ATTENTION TO DETAIL

Purpose

To encourage players to take notice of the small details of team discipline, performance, and presentation that make a difference overall.

Setup

The coach and players sit in a circle near a chalkboard or dry-erase board. The coach talks with players about how winning coaches and winning programs pay significant attention to detail. Few details are left unaddressed. Winners are organized in most aspects of every practice and game.

Run the Drill

1. Coaches and players provide examples of details that teams pay attention to. As they do, a designated writer puts the examples on the board (or each person who thinks of an example can write it down). Here are some ideas:
   - Very specific, planned, and practiced warm-up before a game
   - Organized entrance to the gym
   - Bags carried on the same shoulder
   - Matching practice shirts or shorts or both
   - Matching socks
   - Team meals and possibly team rules during the meal
   - Team presentation
   - Bags lined up the same way at practice and at matches
   - Warm-ups zipped to the same place on each player
   - Chairs lined up perfectly and team bench always clean
   - A specific way to stand in the huddle (e.g., left hand in, right hand on shoulder of player in front)
2. The coach then asks players what they do that is attentive to detail at practice or in games.
3. Players name eight things the team could do to show attention to detail. Some can be things that affect the team's performance; others can be things that players want to do just for fun or to strengthen the team bond.

Coaching Points

- Encourage players to be creative.
- If players have trouble coming up with ideas, offer suggestions.

BE POSITIVE!

Setup

The coach names a player to read a statement about receiving positive comments. The player designated to read the statement appoints a counter. Players sit in a semicircle around the coach, who faces the players.

Run the Drill

1. The player reads this statement: Sometimes, receiving praise (positive pats on the back) from others is more difficult than giving the praise. Let's put Coach on the spot and see how he or she does.
2. The coach stands.
3. One by one, players each make positive statements about the coach. The statements do not need to be in complete sentences and can be about any attribute a player admires or enjoys.
4. The counter keeps track of the number of statements. Players make 25 positive statements about the coach. Optimally, every player will contribute at least one response.
5. Afterward, players discuss how well the coach handled the positive attention and whether it is easier to give or receive praise.

Coaching Point

Extend the conversation by asking players if praise is necessary or beneficial. Ask whether and how players should be given praise during practice and matches. Talk about how it affects performance.

Variation

Choose a player or coach to stand up each day, week, or month to be praised. Sharing kind words to boost self-esteem is an essential element of team building.

RISK CITY

All risks are not wise, but a championship almost always demands that we take risks!

Purpose

To encourage players to discuss risk taking and when it is advisable or necessary in life and in volleyball in order to achieve success.

Setup

One day before the actual activity, the coach asks the team to think of people (a celebrity, professional athlete, or someone who is not famous) who took a big risk to succeed. Players can use an individual, team, or group example. Players have 24 hours to think of examples. The coach prepares examples, too. Just before the activity, the coach and players assemble in a circle.

Run the Drill

1. By turns, players share with the team examples of risk takers. The group discusses each example. The coach contributes examples as needed to keep the conversation flowing.
2. The coach asks questions to direct the discussion.
   Was the risk safe? Worth taking?
   Was there time to think about it before deciding?
   Did the risk directly affect the outcome?
3. The coach steers the conversation to volleyball. The coach asks the following questions:
   Is learning a new skill sometimes a risk?
   Was it a risk for you to play volleyball?
   Is practicing and conditioning all summer a possible risk? If so, how?
   Is playing in a game without being prepared a risk?
   Is serving for an ace a risk when you could easily get a serve in if you are careful?
   Is it a risk to hit down the line when you know you are stronger crosscourt?
   Is it a risk to go for it against a great team that your school or team has never beaten?
   How do we know a good risk? A bad risk?

Coaching Point

Rename your side of the net for one match today or tomorrow Risk City. Discuss the risks the coach and players as individuals or as a team are willing to take today.

YOU WANNA KNOW WHY WE WIN?

Winning coaches are asked a lot of questions, and one of the most frequently asked questions is "Why do you win?" Sharing the answer to that question with players allows them to see through the coach's window—to see themselves through it!

Purpose

To review with players the elements of a winning program and invite discussion as to how your team can achieve success

Setup

The coach creates an outline or list that includes many of the responsibilities of running a volleyball program. Here is a sample outline to get you started:

It Starts With the Coach
Passion for the sport
Knowledge of the sport
Ability to communicate and teach

Recruiting Assistants and Players
Ability to read the game and personalize it
Ability to relate well to others
Ability to assess character and ability

Administrating and Organizing
Preparing, planning, and prioritizing professionally
Deciding on offensive and defensive systems
Selecting players and their assignments
Training, scheduling, strategizing

Coaching
Determining and communicating a philosophy and style
Setting and demanding high standards
Developing volleyball skills and life skills
Teaching, inspiring, and encouraging players to be competitive
Being creative in designing practices and motivating players
Setting up off-court activities for bonding and fun

Communicating
Saying it like it is
Teaching players that winning is the outcome, not the focus
Establishing mutual respect
Presenting a positive attitude and behavior
Making it clear that everyone on the team is special
Embracing change, advancement, and achievement

Public Relations
Serving the community, especially youth
Setting up special appearances for coaches and players
Promoting match attendance
Educating players about public relations

Run the Drill

1. Players sit in circles of 3-4 players. Each is assigned some of the tasks on the list.
2. One player from each group writes down the ideas the players generate about what is involved in each task. For example, for embracing change, advancement, and achievement; players might list ideas such as the following: In order to be a better team, we need to try new skills, new drills, and believe in our coach. In order to win conference, we must practice harder than the others.

Coaching Points

- Focus on the roles you feel players are most in need of recognizing. Emphasize the information that is most likely to benefit your players.
- Invite players to share their thoughts during the outlined discussion.

WINNERS AND WHINERS

Purpose

To provide an understanding of the makeup of winners and whiners and to shift the conversation away from the concept of *winners and losers*.

Setup

Players gather around the coach, who reads the following statement:

It is uncommon to find someone who chooses to be a loser in life! Imagine someone thinking, "Oh, I sure hope my tire is flat today," or "I hope I get a speeding ticket on the way to school," or "I am certainly hoping I am last in the race today." We want to be winners. We don't choose to be losers. But we do make a decision, even if we are unaware of it, to live life as winners or as whiners!

There are many characteristics of winners and whiners. A team built with many winning characteristics is naturally going to be stronger than a team with whining characteristics. A winner is not defined simply by the scoreboard. A winner is defined by having many of the characteristics that we expect of a champion.

Run the Drill

1. The coach gives an example or two of the characteristics of winners and of whiners. To begin, the coach says, "Winners *give* a pat on the back. Whiners *ask for* a pat on the back." After a couple of statements, players should be able to see the difference.

2. The coach then offers a couple of contrasting scenarios: Imagine a player who shanks a pass into the stands and then mopes, lowering and shaking his or her head, so that teammates will come over to console the player. Now imagine a player who makes the same error and keeps his or her head up for the team and actually offers a hand to another so as to "shake it off" before the next play begins.

3. Once players have the idea, the coach asks for examples from the team.

Coaching Points

- Post the Winner and Whiner list where the players can see it to offer a reminder to all.
- Watch for opportunities to drive the message home in practice. When a whining moment occurs, ask how it might be changed to a winning moment. Ask how a winner would respond. Repeatedly pointing out even the slightest whines and changing them on the spot makes a remarkable difference in the attitude of the team and in the lives of the individuals.

Winners	Whiners
Are positive	Are negative
Pay attention	Want attention
Are detail orientated	Are need oriented
Are focused; have a solid sense of direction	Are unfocused; have no sense of direction and won't ask
Have a can-do attitude (Whatever it takes)	Have a can't-do attitude (Whatever)
Accept change	Reject change
Have high expectations	Have low or no expectations
Critique	Criticize
Give a pat on the back	Ask for a pat on the back
Are all about the *team*	Are all about *me*
Have a work ethic that matters	Put forth a weak effort that matters not
Surround themselves with winners and *wannabewinners*	Surround themselves with whiners and *wannabewhiners*
Rest	Don't wake up
Think *win*	Think *whine*
Give	Take

CELEBRITY DOUBLE TROUBLE

This is a great game for long van or bus rides because it can last a long time.

Purpose

To get players involved in a fun team activity in which volleyball is *not* the focus.

Setup

The coach divides the team into two groups. Each group sits in a small circle next to the other group.

Run the Drill

1. The first person in one circle says the name of a celebrity.
2. The first person in the other circle thinks of a celebrity whose *first* name starts with the initial letter of the last name of the celebrity the other group just gave.
3. If someone in the group yells a name with the same initial in both the first and last name, such as Barry Bonds, then the other group must come up with a "double name" that also starts with the same letter (e.g., Bob Barker). The "double name" pattern continues until the end of the game.
3. Players can use any famous name from sports, music, acting, or politics. They cannot use a friend's name. Here's an example:

   Group A starts with Chipper Jones. Group B responds with John Smoltz (using the J from Jones as the first letter of the celebrity's first name).

   Group A says Sam Snead. Because this is a double, the other team must say an S-S name or they lose the round.

4. Play continues until a team is stumped. The winner gets to start again with a celebrity name.

Coaching Point

Playing volleyball calls for quick thinking and quick responding. Have fun with this game!

Variation

Limit the names to a particular category, gender, or sport.

About the AVCA

The mission of the American Volleyball Coaches Association (AVCA) is to advance the sport of volleyball and its coaches. The vision of the AVCA is for volleyball to become a mainstream sport in America and for the AVCA to be the epicenter for leadership, advocacy, and professional development.

The AVCA was incorporated as a private nonprofit educational corporation in 1981. The AVCA currently has over 5,600 members in all 50 states and the District of Columbia as well as in 30 countries. Eighty percent of college coaches are members of the AVCA, and membership at the high school and club ranks has doubled since 2006. The AVCA provides a professional network for those individuals and companies dedicated to enhancing and promoting the sport. Members include collegiate, high school, club, youth and Olympic coaches, as well as volleyball club directors. The AVCA provides education to volleyball coaches, recognition of elite players and coaches, promotion of volleyball competitions throughout the world, and networking opportunities for volleyball products and service providers. Further information is available at www.avca.org.

About the Authors

Teri Clemens was inducted into the AVCA Hall of Fame in 2004. In 14 years of coaching at Washington University, she compiled an impressive overall record of 529-77 and holds the NCAA DIII record for a career winning percentage of .873. Clemens led the Bears to seven national championships, including an unprecedented six consecutive titles from 1991 to 1996. Recognized as the Tachikara/AVCA DIII Coach of the Year in 1991, 1994, and 1996, Clemens is now a highly sought-after and nationally recognized motivational speaker and clinician. She has received the USA Volleyball All-Time Great Award and is also the author of *Get With It, Girls! Life Is Competition*.

Jenny McDowell is the head coach at Emory University. With a career record of 480-122 and a winning percentage of .800 that ranks fourth all time among DIII coaches, McDowell led Emory to a national championship win in 2008 and a second-place finish in 2010. She was named the AVCA National Coach of the Year in 2008 and the AVCA Regional Coach of the Year in 2004, 2005, and 2008. Before assuming her position with Emory, McDowell was an assistant coach at the University of Georgia, where she helped lead the Bulldogs to a 128-41 record and eight NCAA Tournament appearances. The first and only Georgia volleyball player to have her number retired, McDowell started the Emory Volleyball Camps, which host more than 1,200 campers each summer.